Permission to Pivot

A Simple System for Making Life-Changing Turns

Tom Ferrara

Freiling Agency
www.freilingagency.com

The information in this book is for educational and informational purposes only. The author and publisher make no representations or warranties with respect to the accuracy or completeness of the contents of this work and specifically disclaim all warranties. The advice and strategies contained herein may not be suitable for every situation. Neither the publisher nor the author shall be liable for any loss of profit or any other commercial damages.

Published by Freiling Agency
www.freilingagency.com

ISBN: 978-1-969826-55-9

Printed in the United States of America
First Edition, 2026

Contents

"I refuse to live my life in such a way that one day I may look back and say, 'What if?'"

— Tom Ferrara

What if, Permission to Pivot

A Practical Roadmap for Life-Changing Turns

The world is changing faster than ever. Artificial intelligence is transforming industries, job markets, and even the definition of human value. Millions of people are questioning whether the path they are on still makes sense—or whether they are meant for something more.

In What if, Permission to Pivot, entrepreneur and author Tom Ferrara offers a practical, empowering framework for navigating life's biggest turning points. Through his proven process—**Notice** → **Decide** → **Move** → **Sustain**—you will learn to recognize when it is time to change direction, overcome fear and sunk costs, and create alignment between who you are and what you do.

Whether you are rethinking your career, relationships, health, or purpose, this book is your roadmap to intentional reinvention—so you never have to look back and ask, "What if?"

INTRODUCTION

One Life, Many Turns

It started in the hallways of corporate America—though I didn't exactly belong there.

In my early twenties, I sold computer service contracts door to door in midtown Manhattan. Yes, literally walking—sneaking, usually, into the tailwind of a group of strangers filing into a building—briefcase in hand, trying to convince companies to buy something they didn't think they needed from someone they didn't know.

I'd get thrown out of buildings. Chased by security. I learned which lobbies had cameras and which bathrooms I could disappear into until the guard who'd been called about the unauthorized visitor finally gave up and moved on. I became an expert at reading body language, and at making small talk with receptionists just long enough to get the name of the real decision-maker.

Every "no" became a challenge. Every slammed door was a test of creativity. I learned how to smile through rejection, pivot in real time, and turn cold calls into conversations. It was gritty, humbling, and sometimes absurd—but it taught me lessons I've never forgotten: real rewards come from overcoming obstacles. When something stands in your way or simply stops working, don't quit—figure it out. Life rewards those who keep moving.

And move I did. Within two years, I went from pounding the pavement to running the company—promoted to Interim President at just twenty-five, leading a team of 135 people and steering the business through a successful sale.

It wasn't the product or the service that excited me—it was the process, the challenge. The puzzle of it. The constant adaptation. The game of turning impossible situations into opportunities. Somewhere between being tossed out of another building and landing my first major client, I realized I wasn't just selling contracts—I was building something.

That's when I discovered my true passion: innovation, startups, and growth. The thrill of taking an idea, a product, or a service from nothing to something. The creativity required to find traction where others see only obstacles. The rush of helping a team or a company move from surviving to scaling. That's my fuel. My reward is proving it can be done—and helping others achieve their own passions and goals.

That realization was my first real pivot.

And I have made many since.

Life is not linear. It isn't a straight, predictable path from point A to point B. It's a winding road filled with peaks and valleys, hurdles and detours, surprises and second chances. Above all, life is shaped by our choices.

Every single day, we make hundreds of them.

What do I eat for breakfast? What should I wear? Should I sleep for another hour? Should I call that person back? Why do I feel so restless lately?

Most of these choices feel small, almost automatic. We don't stress over them, and we are often not even conscious that we're making them. Yet every decision nudges us—slightly but surely—in a direction. Taken together, they form the architecture of our lives.

But this book isn't about the small choices.

It's about the big ones.

The moments that don't just nudge you—they redirect you.

The decisions that rewire your path, redefine your identity, and rewrite what's possible.

I call them pivots.

Too many people go through life like hamsters on a wheel—running fast, working hard, doing "all the right things," yet going nowhere new. They convince themselves that their path is predetermined, that they have no choice but to keep doing what they've always done, what their parents did or want them to do, or what others expect of them.

They stay unfulfilled, unchallenged, and unhappy. Worst of all, they convince themselves they don't have the right to change.

But here's the truth: you absolutely have the right to pivot.

When I was twenty-three, I made a promise to myself—one that has guided every major decision I've made since. I wrote it down on the back of my business card while building Remote Lojix:

"I refuse to live my life in such a way that one day I may look back and say, 'What if?'"

That single commitment has pushed me through fear, uncertainty, and every major turn I've ever taken. Because the pain of wondering what might have been is far greater than the discomfort of changing course—or of picking yourself up and dusting yourself off after you've failed at something you were passionate about.

And once you truly internalize that truth, staying the same is no longer an option.

You are not bound by your résumé, your job title, your age, or anyone else's expectations. You get one life —just one. What happens after it, if anything, is unknown. But this life, the one you're living right now, is certain. It is the greatest gift you've been given.

And because it's the only one, it is precious beyond measure.

So the real question is this: if you know your life is precious, why wouldn't you treat it that way? Why wouldn't you allow yourself to course-correct, to choose differently, to pivot—especially when the path you're on no longer feels like yours?

That's what this book is about.

It's a roadmap to help you identify when it's time to change (Notice), make the decision to do something about it (Decide), and take intentional action toward the life you actually want (Move).

Because pivots aren't accidents—they're choices. And while the world notices and sometimes celebrates the "big ones"—the career changes, the relocations, the reinventions—most begin quietly.

They start the same way mine did:

With a moment of awareness.

A flash of truth.

A whisper that says: This isn't it anymore.

The secret to living a life that's truly yours isn't about controlling every outcome—it's about recognizing when it's time to make a turn.

Because one life. Many turns.

The key is knowing when—and how—to take yours.

The First Step: Notice

Every great pivot begins not with a plan, but with awareness. The first step isn't quitting your job or moving across the country—it's noticing the signals that something within you is asking for change.

In the next section, we'll explore how to listen for those signals, interpret what they mean, and uncover the quiet truths hiding beneath your routines.

It's time to wake up to the life you're living—and to the one you're meant to create.

Part One

Notice

Spot the Signals That It's Time to Pivot

Before you can make a pivot, you must first recognize when one is needed. Most people don't miss opportunities because they're not capable—they miss them because they're not paying attention.

Part I is about awareness. It's about tuning into the signals—subtle and loud—that whisper or sometimes shout that your life, your work, or your relationships are misaligned.

This section helps you slow down, observe, and interpret the feedback your life is already giving you. You'll learn how to:

- Measure the hidden costs of "staying the same"
- Assess the true state of your life across multiple domains
- Separate temporary discomfort from deep discontent
- Identify the cravings pointing toward your authentic desires

- View your emotions as powerful, actionable data

When you master the skill of noticing, pivots stop being accidents of crisis and start becoming intentional, empowered choices.

Chapters in Part One

Chapter 1 — The Cost of Staying Still

Chapter 2 — Life Inventory Audit

Chapter 3 — Discontent vs. Discomfort

Chapter 4 — The "Craving" Compass

Chapter 5 — Data in Your Emotions

Chapter One

The Cost of Staying Still

Standing Still Isn't Safe—It's Silently Expensive

"Fine" isn't peace—it's quiet surrender. It's the word we use when we've given up on wanting more.

The Danger of "Fine"

It always starts the same way.

Someone says, "I don't hate my life. I just don't love it."

Or: "It's not that things are bad. They're just... fine."

And that word—fine—is a slow poison.

"Fine" is the justification for inaction, the mask that covers fear. It's how good people talk themselves into staying stuck. There's no urgency in "fine." No alarm. No crisis demanding attention. And that's precisely what makes it so dangerous—it feels manageable even as it quietly erodes everything that matters.

The truth? Standing still isn't safe. It's silently expensive. Every year you remain in a misaligned job, relationship, or mindset, you're paying a hidden tax—one that compounds over time, whether you're tracking it or not.

Most people think standing still is neutral. It isn't. It's decline in disguise.

The Myth of Neutrality

We love to believe that if we "just stay where we are," nothing changes.

"If I keep my head down and keep showing up, things will work themselves out."

But time doesn't pause. The world doesn't wait. Life doesn't get longer.

Doing nothing doesn't freeze the moment—it lets it decay.

Every day you remain stuck, you're trading time—the one resource you will never recover. You can rebuild a business, repair a relationship, recover from financial loss. But you cannot buy back a single hour.

Standing still is like keeping your car in neutral on a hill. You may believe you're holding position, but gravity is already pulling you backward. Slowly. Quietly. Continuously.

When we cling to comfort, what we're really choosing is erosion over evolution.

"Inaction isn't safety—it's slow surrender."

The Opportunity Cost Equation

Economists call it opportunity cost: the price of the options you didn't take.

If you spend an evening scrolling on your phone instead of working on your dream, the cost isn't just the hour you lost—it's what that hour could have created. The same principle applies to your career, your relationships, and your growth.

Staying in a toxic job doesn't just cost you today's stress. It costs you tomorrow's potential—the promotions you didn't pursue, the confidence you didn't build, the options you didn't develop. Remaining in a stagnant relationship doesn't just preserve comfort. It forecloses the possibility of deeper intimacy and genuine expansion.

Every year you delay, the compound interest of lost potential grows. And unlike financial interest, it never refunds.

The Quiet Erosion

The danger of staying still is that it doesn't feel dangerous—at first.

It starts subtly.

You tell yourself you'll make a change "after the holidays." Then, "once things calm down." Then, "when the timing's right." And just like that, someday becomes never.

Monotony chips away at ambition. Routine dulls curiosity. You stop asking, What else might be possible? That's the real cost of stagnation—not just what you lose, but what you stop imagining.

Familiarity masquerades as fulfillment. You confuse comfort with contentment. But familiarity isn't fulfillment—it's safety pretending to be satisfaction. The longer you sit still, the harder it becomes to believe that movement is even possible. And when that belief fades, resignation takes its place.

"The longer you delay your pivot, the quieter your purpose becomes."

The Emotional Cost: Drained Energy, Eroded Confidence

When your outer life doesn't align with your inner truth, something starts leaking.

You wake up tired, even after eight hours of sleep. You need caffeine to start the day and distraction to end it. You tell yourself you're exhausted because you're busy—but deep down, you know the real reason: you're not tired from too much to do. You're tired from not enough meaning.

Every day you perform tasks that don't engage you, your subconscious absorbs a quiet message: This isn't who I'm meant to be. Passion is optional. Survival is enough.

That slow erosion of authenticity kills confidence. You start doubting your instincts. You lose trust in your ability to change. You shrink your goals to fit your current situation—and one day, you realize you've stopped dreaming altogether. The ambitions that once lit you up now feel like relics of a younger, more naive version of yourself. The tragedy isn't that they were impossible. It's that you stopped reaching for them.

The Financial Cost: The Hidden Bill You Don't See

People love to say, "I can't afford to change right now."

But here's the question worth sitting with: Can you afford not to?

Staying in a role beneath your potential is its own form of financial loss. You may have a steady paycheck, but you are under-earning your own capability. You're forfeiting the creativity, promotions, partnerships, and breakthroughs that become available when you're fully alive in your work.

One client of mine stayed in a "safe" corporate role for a decade. It paid well enough. It wasn't miserable. But it also wasn't growing. When she finally made the move to a startup that genuinely excited her, she doubled her income within twenty-four months—not because the market changed, but because she did. She brought her full self to the work, and the work rewarded her for it.

The market doesn't reward complacency. It rewards alignment.

The Regret Premium

There's another bill that comes due eventually—the cost of what if.

I've always said: I refuse to live my life in such a way that one day I may look back and say, "What if?" That's not a mantra—it's a mandate.

Because what if is the most expensive question you'll ever ask yourself.

What if I had taken that risk? What if I'd trusted my gut? What if I'd started when I wanted to, instead of waiting until I had to?

Regret isn't just sadness—it's the interest you pay on deferred dreams. The longer you wait, the heavier it grows.

Psychologist Erik Erikson identified the final stage of human development as a confrontation between Integrity and Despair. In this stage, people look back at their lives and ask the hardest of questions: Did it have meaning? Did I live true to myself? Those who can answer yes tend to experience a sense of wholeness and peace—what Erikson called integrity. Those who cannot are often left with despair: a deep, aching regret over a life that felt misaligned, unlived, or squandered.

Permission to Pivot is a preventative antidote to that despair. It is a proactive framework for the present—for noticing when something feels off, deciding with clarity, and moving toward greater authenticity before you arrive at that final reckoning. Where Erikson's model describes a retrospective confrontation with one's past, this book offers you the tools to shape your future while you still can.

Each pivot, viewed through this lens, becomes an act of integrity: choosing truth over comfort, alignment over inertia. It is the ongoing commitment to becoming the person you were meant to be—not in spite of the turns your life has taken, but because of the courage with which you've navigated them. And even for those who feel they may have already arrived at Erikson's later stage, the principles here can restore meaning, rekindle purpose, and open doors that resignation had closed.

The goal is simple: when you reach the end and look back, may you see a life defined by courage, curiosity, and continual growth—not complacency.

"The pain of change is temporary. The pain of 'What if?' lasts a lifetime."

The Comfort Illusion

Comfort feels good—but that's its trap.

Comfort tells you, "Stay here, you're safe." But safety without growth becomes suffocation. You cannot evolve while standing still. You cannot grow while gripping the past. You cannot pivot without letting go.

The longer you stay comfortable, the smaller your comfort zone becomes. Over time, even modest challenges begin to feel threatening. Eventually, mediocrity itself starts to feel like a risk—and that is when you know the trap has closed.

The Physics of Forward

In physics, an object at rest stays at rest unless acted upon by an outside force. In life, stagnation works exactly the same way.

Once you stop moving, inertia builds. Fear calcifies. The gap between where you are and where you want to be grows wider—and the wider it grows, the more daunting the first step seems.

But here's what's also true: the moment you take even a small step—a single conversation, a phone call, one email sent—momentum begins to build. Action creates clarity. Clarity builds confidence. Confidence fuels more action.

That's how movement begins—not through grand gestures or dramatic declarations, but through consistent, deliberate nudges in the right direction.

The Myth of "The Right Time"

"I'll change when..."

That phrase has derailed more dreams than failure ever will. There is no perfect time. There is only now—and later usually becomes never.

The conditions will not line up perfectly. You will not feel completely ready. The financial situation will always be imperfect. Someone will always need something from you. And that's okay.

Readiness is not something that arrives—it's something you build. Most people who made the pivots they're most proud of will tell you they didn't feel ready. They felt scared. But they moved anyway. And in the moving, they found the footing they'd been waiting for.

The moment you realize the discomfort of staying still outweighs the fear of moving forward—that's your window. Take it.

The Real Risk

Everyone talks about the risk of changing course. Very few people talk about the risk of not changing.

The risk of wasting years while your spirit quietly dulls. The risk of looking back one day and realizing that "good enough" wasn't—not for someone with your gifts, your instincts, your potential. The risk of achieving success on paper while feeling empty at the core.

That is the real danger—the slow death of potential, administered in daily doses so small you barely notice until one day, you do.

> *"You don't avoid risk by standing still. You simply choose a different kind—the risk of never becoming who you could be."*

From Stuck to Starting: The First Movement

If you're reading this and feeling that particular mix of fear and relief—take it as a sign. That sensation is awareness. That is the spark of your pivot.

The next step isn't drastic. It's this: admit that inaction is a decision.

Every day you choose not to change, you are still making a choice—a choice to stay. Bring that decision into the light. Acknowledge it consciously. Name it for what it is. Because once you see it clearly, you can no longer pretend it's neutral. And that recognition—that moment of honest self-awareness—is where every real pivot begins.

That's the power of awareness: it transforms denial into direction.

Reflection Exercise: The Cost Audit

Here is your first tangible step.

Take a notebook and title the page: The Cost of Staying Still. Divide it into three columns:

Area of Life: Where do you feel stuck? (Career, relationship, health, mindset, finances)

Hidden Cost: What is it costing you in time, energy, peace, confidence, joy, or fulfillment?

Opportunity Lost: What possibilities are you forfeiting by staying where you are?

Write honestly. Be uncomfortable. This is your real financial statement of fulfillment.

Once you see those numbers on the page, you'll understand something most people spend decades avoiding: the price of staying is almost always higher than the price of changing.

Closing Thought

Standing still feels safe because it's familiar. But familiarity and fulfillment rarely live in the same neighborhood.

Every day you stay stuck, you pay—in the currency of your potential, your time, and your peace of mind.

Life will always give you reasons to wait. But time will not wait for you.

The question isn't whether staying still costs you something. It's whether you're willing to keep paying the price.

So when you find yourself hesitating, return to this:

"I refuse to live my life in such a way that one day I may look back and say, 'What if?'"

That's not just a quote.

That's your permission to pivot.

Chapter Two

Life Inventory Audit

You Can't Pivot Until You Know Where You Stand

"You can't change what you won't look at."

The Blind Spot Problem

One of the biggest reasons people stay stuck is that they can't see clearly where they actually are.

They know they're frustrated, but can't quite pinpoint why. They feel restless, but can't articulate what's misaligned. They say things like, "I don't hate my life, but something feels off."

That feeling—the quiet discomfort that hums beneath your daily routines—is your internal compass whispering: something needs to change.

But before you can change direction, you must first locate yourself on the map.

This is where most people skip ahead. They jump straight to action—new job, new diet, new partner, new city—without truly understanding what they're trying to fix. That's like trying to navigate without knowing your current coordinates. You'll move, yes, but in circles.

A successful pivot doesn't start with motion. It starts with measurement.

That's what this chapter is about: the Life Inventory Audit—a structured, honest, six-part self-assessment that shines light on the areas of your life most in or out of alignment.

Because clarity always precedes courage.

The Purpose of the Audit

Before you pivot, you have to pause.

This pause isn't procrastination—it's preparation.

You're about to take inventory of your entire life across six domains: **Career**, **Relationships**, **Health**, **Finances**, **Beliefs**, and **Habits**.

Think of it as your personal dashboard. Each domain has a gauge, and when one drops too low, it affects the entire system. Most people don't crash because of one catastrophic failure. They crash because they ignored a dashboard full of blinking warning lights.

This audit helps you spot those warnings before the breakdown.

"Awareness doesn't fix everything—but it's the first step to fixing anything."

The Six Domains of Life Alignment

1. Career: Work That Feeds or Drains You

Your career—or however you spend most of your waking hours—is one of the clearest mirrors of alignment. Ask yourself:

Do I wake up energized by my work, or do I dread Mondays? Do I feel like I'm using my best skills every day, or am I just going through the motions? Is my work meaningful to me, or merely a paycheck? Do I feel seen, challenged, and valued—or invisible and replaceable?

Your career doesn't have to be glamorous to be fulfilling. What matters is whether it aligns with your natural motivations and values. Worth remembering: boredom is not the opposite of stress—misalignment is. If your job drains you more than it develops you, that's not a career—it's a cage.

Score yourself from 1–10. (1 = I'm miserable or disengaged at work. 10 = I'm fully alive, inspired, and aligned with my purpose.) Write that number down.

2. Relationships: The Energy You Keep

You are, as Jim Rohn observed, the average of the five people you spend the most time with. So, who are your five?

Do they elevate you or exhaust you? Support your growth or quietly resent it? Challenge you to rise or keep you comfortably small?

Human beings are emotional ecosystems. The people around you either replenish your energy or deplete it—and this extends well beyond romantic relationships. Your friends, colleagues, mentors, and family dynamics all contribute to the quality of your inner life.

Do you feel emotionally safe with the people closest to you? Do you give and receive encouragement freely? Are you surrounded by people who celebrate your success—or compete with it?

It's not selfish to audit your relationships. It's self-respect.

Score yourself from 1–10. (1 = I feel isolated, unsupported, or drained by those around me. 10 = I'm surrounded by people who energize, support, and uplift me.) Write that number down.

3. Health: The Foundation of Energy

Health isn't just the absence of illness—it's the presence of energy. You can't pivot powerfully if your body is running on fumes.

Do you wake up feeling rested or depleted? Are your daily choices giving you energy or stealing it? Are you fueling your body or numbing it? How often do you move, sweat, or simply breathe deeply?

Physical vitality and emotional clarity are deeply intertwined. A sluggish body creates a sluggish mind. Move a muscle and you change a thought. Health is not about perfection—it's about capacity: your ability to show up fully for your life.

Score yourself from 1–10. (1 = I feel physically drained and out of balance. 10 = I feel vibrant, strong, and consistently energized.) Write that number down.

4. Finances: Freedom or Friction

Money is emotional energy, and few things reveal alignment like your relationship with it.

Finances are not just about income—they're about freedom. The freedom to choose, to pivot, to say yes or no based on desire rather than desperation.

Am I building financial freedom or deepening stress? Do I have clarity around my numbers, or do I practice avoidance? Is my spending aligned with my values or my impulses? Does my financial reality reflect confidence or fear?

This isn't about comparing yourself to others. It's about measuring your sense of agency. Financial stress is one of the loudest forms of emotional noise—it drowns out creativity and amplifies anxiety, making every other domain harder to navigate.

Score yourself from 1–10. (1 = I feel trapped, overwhelmed, or out of control with money. 10 = I feel secure, confident, and in control of my financial path.) Write that number down.

5. Beliefs: The Stories That Shape You

Your beliefs form the blueprint of your reality. They determine what you think you deserve, how far you're willing to reach, and what kind of future you'll allow yourself to imagine.

Do my current beliefs reflect who I am—or who I was told to be? Do I operate from abundance or scarcity? Do I see challenges as opportunities for growth or as punishment? Do I believe I can change—or that I'm permanently stuck as I am?

Many of our deepest beliefs were inherited, not chosen. They arrived in childhood, carried by parents, schools, culture, and old pain. But as an adult, your beliefs are your responsibility. If they're outdated, you're living someone else's script.

Score yourself from 1–10. (1 = My beliefs feel limiting or self-defeating. 10 = My beliefs empower me to grow, take risks, and expand.) Write that number down.

6. Habits: The Daily Proof of What You Value

Habits are where your intentions meet your outcomes. The gap between what you say you want and what your daily behavior actually reflects is one of the most revealing data points in this entire audit.

You can't say you value health and never move. You can't say you want growth and never learn. You can't say you want freedom and fill your calendar with obligations that suffocate you. Your habits are your real priorities—not the ones you post about.

Which daily actions pull you closer to your vision—and which push you away? What do you do every day that aligns with who you want to become? What are you still doing that belongs to an older version of you?

Small habits compound just like small investments. Over time, they either build wealth in your well-being or debt in your dissatisfaction.

Score yourself from 1–10. (1 = My daily habits are inconsistent and misaligned with my goals. 10 = My daily habits consistently support the person I want to become.) Write that number down.

Creating Your Baseline: The Life Dashboard

You now have six numbers—one for each domain. Plot them on a simple wheel, labeling each section with its domain. Draw a dot on each spoke corresponding to your score, then connect the dots.

What you'll see is a visual snapshot of your current alignment. Is your wheel smooth and balanced—or jagged and uneven? Are there areas soaring at 9s and 10s while others hover near 3s and 4s?

That's your roadmap.

A pivot doesn't always mean flipping your entire life upside down. Sometimes it means focusing on one domain—one pressure point of misalignment—and starting there. The goal is not to rebuild everything at once. It's to begin where the need is loudest.

"Awareness creates choice. Choice creates change."

The Power of Honest Measurement

This exercise only works if you tell yourself the truth.

It's tempting to sugarcoat—to give yourself higher marks in areas you know are lagging. But false comfort is the enemy of growth.

Think of this like an X-ray, not a report card. You're not judging yourself. You're diagnosing. There is no shame in the numbers—only information. And information is exactly what you need to move forward.

You can't pivot from a lie.

Why Awareness Hurts (and Why That's Good)

For many people, this exercise stirs real discomfort. You might look at your scores and feel frustrated, disappointed, or even ashamed.

Good. That's the feeling of truth returning to the surface.

Awareness hurts at first because it exposes the gap between where you are and where you could be. But that pain is not punishment—it's potential. It's your brain's way of saying, Pay attention here. And if you lean into it rather than away from it, that same discomfort becomes energy. It becomes movement.

The Pattern That Hides in the Numbers

As you review your scores, you'll likely notice patterns.

Maybe your career is thriving, but your relationships are running on empty. Maybe your habits are disciplined, but your beliefs haven't caught up. Maybe you've built financial security but neglected your health in the process.

Here's what most people miss: imbalance in one domain eventually bleeds into the others. A toxic relationship drains your energy, which affects your health. Poor health lowers your confidence, which limits your ambition. Financial stress strains your relationships, which undermines your happiness. Every domain is connected.

You don't need to fix everything at once—but you do need to understand how everything fits.

"You can't pivot powerfully if half your life is pulling in the opposite direction."

A Personal Story: The Audit That Changed Everything

I've done this audit many times in my own life, and every time it reveals something I wasn't fully seeing.

Years ago, when I was running multiple businesses and wearing the title of "success" like a badge, I sat down to take honest stock. On paper, everything looked strong—revenue up, growth steady, client pipeline full, schedule packed.

But when I scored my six domains, the truth hit hard:

Career: 9. Finances: 8. Relationships: 4. Health: 4. Beliefs: 6. Habits: 5.

A high-performing business. An underperforming life.

That moment forced me to confront what I'd been quietly avoiding: I was building externally while crumbling internally. And that realization—that honest, uncomfortable reckoning with the numbers—became the spark for my next pivot.

I didn't change everything at once. I made one pivot at a time. Here's what each looked like:

The Relationship Pivot: From Presence in Business to Presence in Life

Trigger: A score of 4 in relationships revealed how success had come at the cost of connection.

Shift: From investing all my time and energy into business growth to nurturing the people who mattered most.

Outcome: Rebuilt trust, deeper relationships, and the realization—driven home by coaching youth sports and simply showing up—that true wealth is measured in moments and experiences, in time and attention, not titles or transactions.

The Health Pivot: From Ignoring the Body to Prioritizing It

Trigger: A score of 4 in health exposed the toll of burnout, constant overdrive, lack of exercise, and poor nutrition.

Shift: From pushing my limits to respecting them—incorporating rest, daily movement, and intentional nutrition as non-negotiable components of success.

Outcome: Renewed energy, mental clarity, and a lasting understanding that longevity in business and in life depends on taking care of the vessel that carries you.

The Belief Pivot: From Achievement to Alignment

Trigger: A score of 6 in beliefs revealed that my definition of success was borrowed, not chosen.

Shift: From chasing external validation—valuations, profits, accolades—to anchoring in internal conviction and purpose. My focus moved toward creating real impact: helping clients grow, improving their businesses, and enriching the lives of employees who were just beginning their careers.

Outcome: A more grounded sense of meaning, where success is defined not by comparison but by contribution—the measurable growth of my clients and the lasting difference made in people's lives.

The Habit Pivot: From Reaction to Intention

Trigger: A score of 5 in habits revealed inconsistency and a lack of structure outside of work performance.

Shift: From letting the day dictate my direction to consciously designing routines that supported balance and sustained growth.

Outcome: A stronger daily rhythm, sharper focus, and the lived proof that sustainable change isn't built on willpower—it's built on structure.

How to Read Your Results

Your numbers are not judgments—they're signals.

Low scores (1-4) indicate misalignment or neglect. Start small. Ask: what single change would raise this number by just one point?

Mid scores (5-7) suggest areas that are functional but uninspired—"fine," but not fulfilled. Ask: what would make this area feel truly alive again?

High scores (8-10) reflect genuine strength. But remember: even strengths need maintenance. Neglect a high-scoring area long enough and it will drift.

Your goal isn't perfection—it's awareness. A balanced life is not a static wheel. It's a constantly rotating system, and the key is to keep recalibrating.

Building Your Life Dashboard Routine

Once you've created your Life Dashboard, revisit it quarterly. Just as businesses review their KPIs, treat your personal domains as metrics worth tracking.

Ask: What's improved? What's declined? What new misalignments are beginning to emerge?

This keeps you responsive rather than reactive. Instead of waiting for burnout, breakdown, or crisis to force a pivot, you'll catch drift early—and redirect with intention rather than desperation.

Reflection Exercise: The 10-Minute Audit

Set a timer for ten minutes and complete these steps:

1. List the Six Domains: Career, Relationships, Health, Finances, Beliefs, Habits.

2. Score Each 1–10: Be honest—first instinct only.

3. Identify the Loudest Low: Which domain is draining you the most right now?

4. Write One Sentence: "If I improved this area by a point or two, my life would feel more ______."

That's your first pivot clue. Small awareness. Simple action. Real momentum.

Closing Thought

Most people spend more time planning a week's vacation than they do auditing their own life.

You don't need to wait for a crisis to recalibrate. You just need to look honestly at where you are—and decide that you deserve more than "fine."

This is where pivots begin—not with motion, but with measurement. Because clarity is power. And once you see the truth clearly, you can't unsee it.

"You can't pivot from a place you've never mapped."

CHAPTER THREE

Discontent vs. Discomfort

Learning to Tell Growth from Misfit

"Not all pain means stop. Some pain means you're breaking through."

The Subtle Difference That Changes Everything

There's a quiet but crucial distinction that defines whether your next move is progress or escape—the difference between discomfort and discontent.

Most people confuse them. They feel the tension of change and assume it's a sign they're in the wrong place. But not all pain signals misalignment.

Growth, by nature, is uncomfortable. Misalignment, on the other hand, is intolerable.

Discomfort means you're stretching. Discontent means you're suffocating.

Knowing the difference between the two is the difference between quitting too early and staying too long.

The Growth Zone: When Discomfort Is a Sign You're Evolving

Every meaningful change in your life will begin with discomfort.

Think back to the first time you learned something new—driving a car, starting a job, entering a relationship, even returning to the gym after a long break. You probably felt scared, awkward, anxious, maybe even inadequate.

That's not failure. That's growth friction.

In neuroscience, there's a concept called neuroplastic tension—the mild stress your brain experiences while forming new neural pathways. It's your nervous system learning to adapt. You can't grow without it.

So when you're stepping into something new—a leadership role, a business idea, a healthier relationship dynamic—that tight, uncertain feeling is a good sign. It means you're leaving the known for the possible.

The Hallmarks of Healthy Discomfort

You're likely in the growth zone when:

You feel nervous, but curious. The work challenges you, but you can sense potential on the other side. You doubt yourself at times, but you're still drawn forward. The discomfort feels purposeful—like stretching a muscle that's waking up.

Healthy discomfort often carries a quiet undertone of excitement. Even when it's hard, there's a spark that whispers, this matters.

It might look like: a new business that scares you but feels alive. Speaking up in meetings even though your voice shakes. Saying no to something familiar because you're protecting your future self.

That's expansive pain. It enlarges you, even as it tests you.

"Discomfort is the toll you pay for crossing the bridge to your next chapter."

The Misfit Zone: When Discontent Is a Sign You're Shrinking

Now let's talk about the other kind of pain—the one that doesn't expand you. It erodes you.

Discontent feels different. It's not the sharp pain of stretching—it's the dull ache of stagnation. Like when your leg falls asleep because you've sat too long in a position that no longer fits.

You wake up dreading your day, not because it's hard, but because it's hollow. You go through the motions, check the boxes, nod in meetings—but you feel invisible. Or maybe you wish you were invisible, so you can close your eyes and drift somewhere else entirely.

You know the feeling: the internal countdown during a conference call that won't end, the meeting where twelve people are present and not one of them seems to notice that your spirit left the room twenty minutes ago. Then your name breaks through the fog. You snap back. "Absolutely."

You're not being stretched. You're being squeezed. You're not learning new things—you're unlearning joy.

That's the misfit zone. It's what happens when you're trying to fit yourself into a container that no longer matches your shape.

Maybe it's a job that once challenged you but now just drains you. Maybe it's a relationship that no longer inspires growth, only obligation. Maybe it's a lifestyle that made sense five years ago but feels foreign now.

Discontent is the universe whispering: You've outgrown this.

The Signs of True Misalignment

You're likely in the misfit zone when:

You feel emotionally or physically drained even after rest. You dread routine tasks that once felt rewarding. You feel resentful toward others who seem freer or more fulfilled. You catch yourself fantasizing about escape rather than progress. Your body keeps score—tension, fatigue, headaches, persistent anxiety.

This isn't the pain of growing. It's the pain of staying where you don't belong. You don't need more resilience here—you need a redirection.

"If discomfort stretches you, stay. If it shrinks you, it's time to go."

Why We Confuse the Two

It's easy to mix up discontent and discomfort because both feel uneasy. Both create stress, uncertainty, and resistance.

But here's the difference: one builds you, the other breaks you.

We're wired to avoid pain—any pain. Our brains interpret discomfort as danger. But in modern life, most of what we call danger is actually growth.

That's why so many people quit too early. They walk away from the very thing that's about to unlock their next level—a business idea, a new fitness goal, a hard conversation—because it's uncomfortable. At the same time, others stay far too long in environments that are quietly killing their spirit because it's familiar.

So the real skill isn't endurance or bravery. It's discernment. Learning to ask: Is this pain helping me evolve, or keeping me small?

The Filter Questions

When you're unsure whether to push through or pivot, use these three questions as your compass.

Does this discomfort expand me or deplete me? Growth discomfort feels like tension with purpose. A new manager feels anxious leading a team for the first time—long hours, imposter syndrome—yet deep down knows they're growing into the leader they want to be. The tension has meaning. Misfit discontent, by contrast, feels like emptiness with no direction: a seasoned professional wakes up dreading work every day, not because it's demanding, but because there's no spark—

just a quiet sense that this isn't what they're meant to be doing.

Will this challenge lead to growth or just more frustration? Growth pain leads somewhere—you see glimpses of progress. Discontent loops endlessly: no matter how much effort you put in, nothing fundamentally changes.

Am I excited by the possibility beyond the pain, or do I see no light at all? Growth always carries a spark, even a faint one. If you can't see any possibility—only exhaustion—it's time to reassess.

The answers won't always be immediate. But if you sit with them honestly, they'll reveal your truth.

A Personal Example: The Pivot Trigger

When I sold my company years ago, I stayed on as an executive through the acquisition. On paper, it was a dream scenario—title, strong salary, stability, the respect of my peers.

But over time, I started to feel a creeping discontent. At first, I mistook it for discomfort. "Maybe I just need to adjust," I told myself. "New structure, new rules, new culture—it's an adaptation period."

But months passed, and that feeling didn't fade. It grew.

I realized it wasn't growth tension—it was a slow loss of alignment. I was no longer building. I was managing. I wasn't creating; I was maintaining. The work was steady, but my energy wasn't.

That's when I knew: I wasn't meant to endure this. I was meant to evolve from it.

That awareness—that distinction between discomfort and discontent—gave me permission to pivot again.

"You can't build your future while defending your past."

The Biology of Growth Pain

Your brain is designed for safety, not success.

When you step into anything new, your nervous system sounds the alarm: This is unfamiliar. This could go wrong. That alarm feels the same whether you're quitting a job, starting a business, or simply trying to speak up in a meeting.

But familiarity and safety are not the same thing. In fact, familiarity often keeps you trapped in a known pain you've simply learned to tolerate.

The key is to reinterpret the signal. When discomfort arises, ask: Is this fear because I'm in danger, or because I'm expanding? Nine times out of ten, it's the latter.

The Emotional Treadmill

People stuck in misfit discontent often experience what psychologists call learned helplessness—the belief that nothing they do will change their situation.

So they stop trying. They stop hoping. They go to work, come home, scroll, sleep, repeat. Their energy isn't being spent—it's being absorbed by a life that doesn't fit.

The longer you live there, the more you internalize the lie that you can't change. That's why recognizing discontent early is crucial. It's not just emotional—it's existential.

How to Listen to Your Signals

Your body knows before your mind does.

When you're in growth discomfort, your energy feels electric—nervous, but alive. When you're in discontent, your body feels heavy, tight, sluggish, resistant.

Start observing your physical cues. Do you feel energized after challenge, or depleted? Do you feel excited before new opportunities, or dread? Do you feel curiosity, or numbness? Your nervous system keeps score. Trust it.

The Pivot Spectrum

Think of your experience on a spectrum with four zones:

The Comfort Zone feels safe but stagnant—it's time to stretch. The Growth Zone (Discomfort) feels uncertain but alive—lean in. The Misfit Zone (Discontent) feels draining and shrinking—step out. The Burnout Zone feels numb and detached—recover first, then redirect.

You don't need to fear discomfort. But you must respect discontent. Because ignoring it doesn't make it go away—it just hardens into regret.

*"Discomfort says: You're evolving.
Discontent says: You're disappearing.
Know the difference."*

Don't Quit Growth Prematurely

Some people pivot too soon.

They mistake growth discomfort for misalignment and abandon the very thing that's about to pay off. They quit the business when it's about to break through. They stop the habit when results are just beginning. They leave the relationship right before honest communication could transform it.

True growth always passes through resistance. If you quit the moment you feel friction, you'll spend your life restarting instead of arriving.

So before you leave, pause and ask: Am I leaving because this is wrong for me, or because it's stretching me? If the answer is stretching, stay. If the answer is shrinking, go.

Don't Romanticize Struggle Either

The opposite trap is just as dangerous—staying in misalignment because you think endurance equals strength.

You tell yourself: every job has bad days. Relationships take work. I just need to be more grateful. And yes, all of that can be true.

But there's a difference between effort and erosion. Effort builds resilience. Erosion builds resentment.

Staying where you don't belong isn't loyalty—it's self-abandonment.

The Golden Middle: Where Growth and Alignment Meet

When you find the sweet spot—the intersection of meaningful discomfort and aligned purpose—life feels different.

You wake up challenged but fulfilled. Tired but proud. Uncertain but alive. That's the zone of sustainable growth: not easy, but energizing.

This is where pivots lead when done right. You're not escaping something—you're evolving into something better.

Reflection Exercise: Your Growth or Misfit Map

Grab your journal or open your notes app.

For each major area of your life—Career, Relationships, Health, Finances, Beliefs, Habits—answer the following: Where do I currently feel uncomfortable? Is that discomfort stretching me (growth) or draining me (misfit)? What small sign tells me which it is—excitement or exhaustion? What would happen if I leaned in for thirty more days? What would happen if I didn't?

This exercise builds emotional intelligence: the ability to listen to your internal data instead of reacting blindly to discomfort.

Closing Thought

The next time you feel friction, don't rush to label it as wrong.

Pause. Breathe. Ask what kind of pain it is.

Because pain isn't always a punishment—sometimes it's an invitation. An invitation to grow. Or an invitation to go.

The wisdom lies in knowing which one you've been given.

CHAPTER FOUR

The Craving Compass

Your Desires Aren't Random—They're Data

> *"The things you daydream about aren't distractions. They're directions."*

The Signal in Longing

There's a quiet signal inside every human being—a pulse of wanting that flickers beneath the noise of daily life. You feel it when your mind drifts mid-meeting, or when you catch yourself imagining a different kind of day, a different kind of work, a different version of you.

Most people dismiss those moments as distractions, fantasies, or guilt-inducing indulgences. Snap out of it, they tell themselves. Get back to reality.

But what if those moments of longing are reality—just not the one you're living yet? What if those recurring visions, those pangs of envy, those whispers of I wish I could... are not random at all? What if they're your inner compass trying to point you home?

The Truth About Craving

We've been taught to distrust desire. We call it selfish, unrealistic, immature. We've been told that contentment is virtue, that wanting more is greed.

But there's a difference between greed and growth.

Greed says: I need more to be enough. Growth says: I sense there's more in me to express.

One is hunger for accumulation. The other is hunger for alignment.

Your cravings—the ones that keep showing up—aren't accidents. They're feedback loops from your deeper self. They're evidence that part of you knows there's more available than what you've been settling for.

"Longing is the language of the life you haven't lived yet."

The Biology of Desire

Desire isn't weakness. It's wiring.

Neuroscientists call it the seeking system—a network in the brain that drives curiosity, motivation, and goal pursuit. When activated, it releases dopamine not as a reward for achieving something, but as energy for moving toward something.

That means desire itself—not fulfillment—is what fuels growth. So when you feel a pull toward a new idea, career, or way of living, your biology is literally signaling: Move this way.

Suppressing that instinct is like ignoring your GPS because you're afraid to leave the driveway.

When Your Mind Wanders, Pay Attention

Have you ever noticed where your mind goes when you're not forcing it to focus?

In moments of stillness—in the shower, on a walk, during a long drive home—your brain reveals what it's craving. That's not laziness. That's truth without censorship.

When your mind drifts toward teaching, building, writing, designing, helping, or leading—that's data. Those aren't fantasies; they're feedback. Most people treat daydreams like background noise, but they're more like pings from your subconscious: This is what aliveness feels like.

If daydreams are your inner compass, envy is its highlighter. Where longing quietly points toward what's missing, envy underlines it in bold. It draws your attention to the areas where your potential is calling but your reality hasn't caught up. And if you're willing to look past the guilt and comparison, envy can reveal what your heart has been trying to tell you all along.

The Envy Exercise

Envy gets a bad reputation. We're taught to feel ashamed of it—to hide it under politeness or denial. But envy, used consciously, is one of the most accurate emotional instruments you have.

Behind envy is admiration in disguise. Every time you feel a pang of it toward someone, your psyche is saying: They have something I want to develop in myself.

So instead of suppressing envy, study it. Take out a notebook and list the people who trigger it—personally or professionally. Then for each name, ask: What specifically do I envy about them? Their freedom? Their impact? Their creative expression? Their confidence? What does their life represent that mine doesn't yet?

Patterns will emerge. You might realize it's not about money—it's about autonomy. Not about fame—it's about being seen for your authentic voice. Not about their business—it's about owning your time.

However, if what you envy is purely material—the house, the car, the jewelry—pause before you pivot. That kind of envy isn't pointing you toward purpose; it's pointing you toward comparison. There will always be someone with a bigger home or a flashier life. Chasing that creates motion, not meaning.

Use envy as a compass for becoming, not competing.

A Personal Story: The Daydream That Built a Company

Years ago, while taking a break from entrepreneurship, I was working inside a large college system. On paper, it was everything I thought I wanted—stable, respected, with a clear sense of security.

But during meetings, as I watched outside agencies control the marketing spend—opaque reports, rising costs, no real accountability, zero innovation—my mind kept wandering. Why is it being done like this? Why do the people spending the money have the least control over it? Why isn't there transparency? Why isn't this information instant?

For months, I brushed it off. Be grateful. Don't rock the boat. But that whisper wouldn't leave. It followed me home, into the shower, on my drives to work. Eventually, I realized it wasn't noise—it was direction.

That recurring daydream became a blueprint, and that blueprint became a company: CUnet—built on transparency, performance, and trust. From start to sale, in less than two and a half years, that whisper of longing had grown into a mid-eight-figure outcome.

That's the power of craving when you finally stop treating it as distraction and start recognizing it as direction. The whispers don't go away when you ignore them. They wait patiently until you're ready to listen.

"Your cravings are coded messages from your future self."

Why We Resist Our Own Desires

We fear our cravings because they disrupt the status quo.

Desire reveals the gap between where we are and where we want to be. And that gap can be painful to look at. It forces a confrontation: If this isn't what I want, why am I still here?

So instead, we hide behind rationalizations: I'm lucky to have this. It's too late to change. Other people would do anything for this life.

Those statements sound noble, but they're fear in polite disguise. Gratitude is healthy. Settling is not. You can be grateful for what you have and still crave more.

You can appreciate your chapter and still want to grow into the next.

That's not discontent. That's evolution.

Cravings Are Maps, Not Mandates

Not every desire is meant to be acted on immediately. Some are directional, not destination-based.

Maybe your craving to live by the ocean isn't literal —it's your soul craving peace, space, and simplicity. Maybe your envy of an artist isn't about painting—it's about freedom of expression. Maybe your daydream of running a business isn't about money—it's about autonomy and ownership.

Your cravings may not tell you exactly what to do next, but they will tell you where to look. Follow the feeling, not the form.

From Fantasy to Framework: Turning Cravings into Clarity

Once you've gathered your data—your envies, your daydreams, your desires—it's time to translate them into insights.

Ask yourself: What do all these cravings have in common? Look for repeating themes: freedom, creativity, impact, challenge, adventure, peace.

What are these desires trying to tell me about who I'm becoming? You might find that your cravings aren't about escaping—they're about expanding.

What one small experiment could I try to honor this craving? Want to write? Start a weekly blog. Want to travel? Plan one local trip this month. Want to mentor others? Offer one person guidance. Cravings become clarity through contact—you must engage with them to understand them.

How to Read Your Compass

The Craving Compass has four signals, each pointing toward something specific.

Recurring daydreams are your subconscious testing possibilities—journal them and prototype small versions. Envy is admiration in disguise—study and emulate the quality, not the person. Boredom is energy looking for a new outlet—identify where you've outgrown your environment. Excitement is an alignment preview—follow and explore it intentionally.

The rule is simple: if it keeps returning, it's real. If it excites you and scares you, it's calling. If it drains you to ignore it, it's overdue.

You don't need to overhaul your life tomorrow. You just need to stop pretending you don't know what you want.

The Cost of Ignoring the Compass

When you silence your cravings, you silence your creativity. You become numb—not because life is bad, but because you've stopped letting yourself want.

Desire is what animates us. It's the pulse of potential. When you suppress it, life turns gray.

Oscar Wilde once observed that there are only two tragedies in life: not getting what one wants, and getting it. I'd add a third: stopping wanting altogether. That's when people start calling their lives "fine."

And we already know what "fine" costs you.

Reflection Exercise: The Desire Decoder

Spend fifteen quiet minutes with a pen and paper. Answer the following prompts:

List three people you admire or envy. What specifically about their life or character do you long for?

List five daydreams or "what ifs" that keep resurfacing. For each, ask: What quality of life am I actually craving here? Freedom, recognition, creativity, passion, peace, contribution?

Circle the top two that feel the strongest and ask: What small step could I take this month to explore this energy?

Don't rush to make it a plan. Just let it inform your awareness. The goal isn't action yet. The goal is alignment.

Closing Thought

Your cravings are not random. They are your roadmap.

Each wish, each spark of envy, each recurring daydream—all of it is feedback.

So the next time you find yourself staring out the window, imagining something different, don't dismiss it.

Listen. That's your inner compass trying to show you the way. You don't have to know every turn. You just have to be willing to take one.

"The life you crave is not a coincidence. It's a calling."

Chapter Five

Data in Your Emotions

Your Feelings Are Feedback, Not Flaws

"Emotions are not interruptions in your story. They're instructions for your next move."

The Myth of "Good" and "Bad" Emotions

We grow up learning to sort emotions into two boxes: good and bad.

Happiness, excitement, confidence? Good. Anxiety, boredom, dread? Bad.

We're taught to chase the first and avoid the second. But in doing so, we've misunderstood one of life's most intelligent systems.

Emotions aren't moral. They're informational. They are data points from your inner world—metrics that tell you where your life is in or out of alignment. Your emotions are not random mood swings; they're your body's way of whispering: Something needs your attention.

When you learn to read those signals accurately, you stop being controlled by them and start being guided by them.

The Emotional Dashboard

Imagine your emotional system like the dashboard of a car.

When a light turns on—low fuel, check engine, low tire pressure—you don't panic and throw out the car. You don't shame the dashboard. You recognize it as information. It's not saying something's wrong with you; it's saying something needs attention.

Boredom, dread, anxiety—these are emotional dashboard lights. They don't mean you're broken. They mean your internal systems are giving you feedback.

The problem is most of us were never taught how to interpret those lights. We ignore them, suppress them, or catastrophize them. This chapter will help you do something different: read them like data.

"Your feelings are facts about your needs."

Boredom: Lack of Growth

Boredom isn't laziness. It's lack of expansion.

It's your mind's way of saying: I've mastered this level—what's next? You can tell you're in a boredom loop when you find yourself endlessly scrolling, half-working, half-thinking—filling time but not fueling purpose.

Most people interpret boredom as a personal flaw: Why can't I just be content? But contentment and stagnation are not the same thing. Contentment is satisfaction with progress. Stagnation is the absence of it. You are wired for growth. When you stop growing, your energy naturally dips.

Psychologists define boredom as the unmet need for meaningful challenge. When the brain is under-stimulated—when it's no longer required to stretch, create, or explore—dopamine drops. Your system goes on standby. That's why boredom feels heavy and dull: it's not depression; it's deprivation. You're craving novelty, learning, and forward motion.

Next time you feel bored, don't shame it—question it. Ask: What part of me is underused right now? Where in my life am I no longer being challenged? What's one area I could expand, learn, or stretch?

A Personal Story: The Day Boredom Spoke Up

I'll never forget a moment from high school.

I was a sophomore—a big football player—sitting in geometry class, a class that felt like slow motion. The teacher was walking the aisles as he lectured. Without thinking, I started running my pencil up and down the spiral of my notebook, that slow shhhk-shhhk-shhhk filling the quiet room.

He slammed his hand down on my desk. "Stop doing that! Why are you doing that?"

Without thinking, I blurted out: "Because I'm bored."

The class went silent. He sent me straight to the principal's office. But instead of getting in trouble, the principal listened, looked at my grades, and moved me into the higher-level math class.

That day I learned something important: boredom isn't laziness. It's a signal. It's your brain saying, I've mastered this level. I'm ready for more.

"Boredom isn't the absence of interest. It's the absence of impact."

Dread: Misalignment

If boredom whispers, dread shouts.

Dread is that pit in your stomach when you wake up and remember what's waiting for you—the meeting you can't stand, the job that drains you, the relationship that feels heavy. Dread isn't a signal to toughen up. It's a signal that something in your environment is deeply misaligned with who you are.

If boredom is a nudge, dread is an alarm.

When you consistently feel dread toward something, it's because your nervous system recognizes it as unsafe or unfulfilling. You can fake enthusiasm for a while. You can rationalize or justify. But your body doesn't lie. Dread doesn't come from hard work—it comes from the wrong work. It's the emotional tax you pay for staying where you no longer fit.

Don't confuse dread with resistance, either. Resistance says: This is hard. Dread says: This is wrong. You might resist going to the gym but feel proud afterward—that's discomfort. You might dread walking into your office and feel empty afterward—that's misalignment. One drains your energy in anticipation; the other replenishes it after completion.

When you feel that heaviness, ask: What part of me feels trapped right now? Is this dread occasional (resistance) or chronic (misfit)? What specific moments or tasks trigger it most? What does my body want instead—relief, rest, or redirection?

Clarity here matters. Because dread left unchecked turns into burnout. And burnout isn't only caused by too much to do—it's often caused by too much that doesn't matter.

"Discipline feels like effort. Dread feels like erosion."

Anxiety: Unmet Need for Safety or Change

Anxiety is one of the most misunderstood emotions.

We think of it as an enemy—something to be medicated, numbed, or conquered. But anxiety, like all emotions, carries a message. It's not random static in your system. It's data about your needs.

Sometimes anxiety means you're unsafe—physically, mentally, emotionally, or financially. Other times, it means you're stagnating and your soul is suffocating. Either way, it's asking for change. A pivot.

There are two kinds worth distinguishing. Protective anxiety keeps you safe—like when your intuition warns you about a situation or person that doesn't feel right. Progressive anxiety arises when you're about to grow—when you're stepping into the unknown, taking risks, confronting truth. Both are signals, but their actions differ. Protective anxiety says: Pause. Reassess safety. Progressive anxiety says: Proceed. You're expanding.

The trick is learning to tell which is which.

Here's the key: your brain can't tell the difference between a real threat and a perceived one. It processes public speaking and a charging tiger through the same alarm system. That means your anxiety might not be warning you of danger—it might just be announcing change.

Reframe it like this: This isn't fear of danger—it's energy for direction.

Reframing Emotions: From Judgment to Data

Most people spend their lives trying to manage or mute their emotions.

They distract, overwork, overeat, or over-rationalize instead of asking: What are you trying to tell me? But emotions aren't meant to be managed—they're meant to be interpreted.

Here's the reframe that changes everything. When you feel boredom, the old story says: I'm ungrateful. The new interpretation: I've stopped growing. When you feel dread: not I'm weak, but I'm misaligned. When you feel anxiety: not I'm broken, but something needs safety or change. When you feel restlessness: not I can't focus, but there's unrealized potential inside me. When you feel frustration: not I'm failing, but I care deeply and something isn't matching that.

Emotional intelligence isn't the absence of emotion—it's the mastery of meaning.

"Your emotions are not problems to solve. They're patterns to understand."

A Personal Story: The Meeting I Couldn't Ignore

There was a period when I was in a role that looked ideal on paper. The title was impressive. The compensation was solid. The company had momentum.

But every week, there was this one recurring meeting that I dreaded. It wasn't because of the workload or the people. It was because every time I sat in that room, I felt disconnected from purpose.

I realized that feeling wasn't about the meeting—it was about the meaning. It was my system saying: You're done here.

I tried to ignore it for months. But dread only grows louder when ignored. Eventually, that single recurring feeling became the catalyst for my next pivot.

That's how it often works. It's not the big moments that signal change. It's the quiet repetition of emotion that refuses to fade.

The Three Metrics of Emotional Alignment

When you begin listening to your emotions instead of fighting them, three clear metrics emerge—just like data points on a dashboard.

Energy: How do I feel after? Energized or depleted? **Meaning:** Does this activity or relationship feel purposeful or pointless? **Anticipation:** Do I look forward to it or dread it?

These three indicators will tell you faster than any spreadsheet whether something belongs in your life.

Reflection Exercise: Your Emotional Dashboard

Grab your journal or open your notes app and write:

List three emotions you've felt most consistently this month. For each, write what situations trigger it most often. Then ask: What might this emotion be trying to tell me?

Finally, write one micro-action that would honor that information—a boundary to set, a conversation to have, a change to make, or a rest to take.

Example: Emotion: dread before Monday meetings. Message: this job is misaligned with my values. Action: schedule one networking call this week to explore alternatives.

You don't have to overhaul your life overnight. You just have to start listening.

"When you learn to read your emotions, confusion becomes clarity—and clarity becomes courage."

Closing Thought

Your emotions are not inconveniences. They're intelligence.

They are your soul's metrics—real-time feedback on your alignment with your truth.

Boredom says: Grow. Dread says: Change. Anxiety says: Listen.

Each one is a signal guiding you closer to the life you're meant to live.

So the next time you feel a surge of emotion, don't shut it down.

Pause. Observe. Interpret.

Because in that moment, your inner dashboard isn't malfunctioning—it's messaging you.

And if you pay attention, it will show you exactly where to turn next.

PART TWO

Decide

Grant Yourself Permission

Awareness alone doesn't change your life. You can notice every signal, audit your life, and even crave something different—yet still stay stuck. Why? Because the hardest part of a pivot is not external. It's internal.

Part II is about decision-making. It's about giving yourself the permission you've been waiting for—whether from society, parents, bosses, or your own inner critic. You'll learn to dismantle the myths that chain you to your past, confront and budget your fears, separate your identity from your current labels, craft a clear pivot thesis, and free yourself from the need for external validation.

This section equips you with the mental frameworks and decision tools to stop circling the "should I/shouldn't I" loop and finally step forward with conviction.

CHAPTERS IN PART TWO

Chapter Six

Smashing the Sunk-Cost Myth

Your Past Is Tuition, Not a Prison

"You don't owe your future to your past—only to your potential."

The Trap of "I've Come Too Far"

At some point, everyone faces the same haunting thought: But I've already put too much into this to walk away.

You've invested years in a career, a relationship, or a degree. You've sacrificed weekends, money, and sleep. You've built an identity around it and told people, This is who I am. And even when that identity no longer fits, you stay—because leaving feels like betraying your past self.

That's the sunk-cost trap. It's the quiet illusion that the time, energy, or money you've already spent should dictate the rest of your life.

But here's the truth: yesterday's decisions don't justify tomorrow's unhappiness.

The Psychology Behind the Trap

Behavioral economists call it the sunk-cost fallacy—the tendency to continue a behavior simply because we've already invested in it, even when the future payoff no longer makes sense.

You see it everywhere. The investor who keeps throwing money into a failing position—what traders call catching a falling knife. The couple who stays together "because it's been ten years." The employee who won't leave because they've been there this long.

We think quitting means wasting the past. But in reality, continuing means sacrificing the future.

"The cost of staying stuck is always higher than the price of starting over."

The Airport Gate Analogy

Imagine you're at the gate for a flight that keeps getting delayed. First thirty minutes. Then an hour. Then another. You've been there six hours.

The gate agent says, "We still don't know when it will take off." What do most people do? They keep waiting—because they've already waited so long. But does the fact that you've waited make waiting longer any smarter? The rational choice is to find another route.

That's what the sunk-cost trap looks like in real life. We wait at emotional gates—jobs, degrees, relationships—telling ourselves, Maybe it'll take off soon. But deep down, we already know: the gate isn't the problem. The refusal to move on is.

Why We Stay Even When We Know

We don't cling to the past because it's logical. We cling because it's familiar. Walking away feels like admitting failure—like letting go of an identity we worked hard to earn.

Three forces keep us locked in place. The first is **ego investment**. We don't just invest money or time—we invest identity. When your title or reputation is tied to what you've built, changing course can feel like erasing who you are. But evolution isn't erasure; it's expansion. You're not deleting your past—you're upgrading its purpose.

The second is **fear of judgment**. What will people think? What if they say I wasted my degree? The truth is that people might talk for five minutes, then go back to worrying about their own lives. Don't trade decades of fulfillment for five minutes of other people's opinions.

The third is **hope addiction**. We keep telling ourselves it'll get better. And sometimes it does. But often, that hope isn't faith—it's fear in disguise. Hope becomes a habit that postpones truth. If you've been saying "just a little longer" for years, that's not patience. That's denial.

The Past Is Tuition

Every mistake, every chapter, every investment—none of it is wasted. It's tuition.

You paid for lessons. You earned experience. You built wisdom. The tragedy isn't in moving on—the tragedy is refusing to use what you've learned because you're too loyal to the classroom you've outgrown.

That law degree taught you how to think critically. That failed business taught you resilience. That heartbreak taught you boundaries. Nothing was wasted. It was all training.

"You don't lose the value of your past by pivoting—you cash it in."

Real-World Pivots

Consider Howard Schultz. He worked as Director of Retail Operations for a small Seattle company called Starbucks—which at the time sold only coffee beans and equipment, not brewed coffee. On a business trip to Italy, Schultz encountered the café culture: espresso bars as community hubs. He couldn't shake the vision of coffee as connection, not just commodity. When the founders rejected his idea, he left to start his own concept, then bought Starbucks and reimagined it as the global coffeehouse we know today. He pivoted from employee to entrepreneur, from selling beans to creating experiences.

Vera Wang spent her youth as a competitive figure skater and later became an editor at Vogue. When she failed to make the U.S. Olympic team, she faced an identity crisis. At forty, frustrated by the lack of stylish bridal gowns while planning her own wedding, she designed her own—and launched Vera Wang Bridal despite having no formal design training. Her background as an athlete and editor gave her a unique eye for form and detail. She became one of the world's most influential designers by refusing to let one closed door define her story.

Lesser-known pivots are even more common. Mark spent twelve years as a corporate auditor—steady, respected, and quietly miserable. A chance encounter with a career assessment pointed him toward creative communication and storytelling. He started writing at night, attended workshops, and eventually left finance entirely. Today he's a published novelist. His accounting background gave him the discipline to finish what he started; his pivot gave him a reason to.

A lawyer who spent twelve years in corporate litigation realized her favorite part of the job was mentoring interns. She left her six-figure role to teach high school. Her courtroom experience didn't vanish—it made her an extraordinary teacher who trained students to think critically and argue well.

A senior executive with the corner office and the title developed chest tightness his doctor traced directly to chronic stress. He pivoted into wellness coaching. He earns less per quarter but measures richness differently now—by energy, peace, and presence with his family.

Each of these people heard the same inner voice: But I've already invested too much. Each arrived at the same realization: the true waste would have been staying.

The Opportunity-Cost Equation

Here's a practical exercise to break the sunk-cost spell.

Write down the sentence that keeps you stuck: "But I've already invested too much in _______." Now answer honestly: How many years have you given this? What have those years cost you in joy, energy, health, or peace? What will another five years cost if nothing changes?

Now flip it: What could those same five years create if you redirected your energy toward something aligned?

That's your real equation. Because the question isn't What will I lose if I leave? It's What will I lose if I stay?

"Your time is a non-refundable currency. Spend it where it multiplies."

Why Staying Feels Safer

The brain craves certainty. Familiar pain feels safer than unfamiliar possibility.

That's why even miserable situations feel "comfortable"—your nervous system has adjusted to them. When you consider leaving, your brain floods with anxiety: unknown territory detected. But fear of change doesn't mean change is wrong. It means you're leaving the known for the necessary.

Safety is not the same as satisfaction. You can be safe and miserable, or uncertain and alive.

The Courage to Cut the Rope

Picture a hot-air balloon straining against its tethers. It can only rise as high as the ropes allow.

Your sunk costs are those ropes—old commitments, outdated beliefs, expired dreams. You don't cut them because they were mistakes. You cut them because you're ready to rise. Letting go isn't disrespect to your past self—it's obedience to your future self.

The 5-Year Projection

Try this. Imagine your life exactly as it is—same work, same routine, same feeling—for the next five years. Write a short paragraph describing how that looks and feels. Be brutally honest.

Now imagine you made a bold move today toward something you truly want. Write a paragraph about how that version of you feels after five years.

Compare the two. Which life feels heavier? Which feels lighter? The weight in your body as you read those paragraphs will tell you more truth than any spreadsheet ever could.

"Regret weighs tons. Fear weighs ounces.
Choose what you can carry."

A Personal Story: The Lesson of Letting Go

When I sold my company, I had to face this myth head-on.

I'd built it from scratch—poured years of effort, creativity, and sleep deprivation into it. It was my identity, my proof of worth. But after the acquisition, something shifted. I was no longer building; I was maintaining. The thrill was gone, and so was the alignment.

Yet I hesitated, because every time I thought about moving on, that voice whispered: But you've worked too hard to let it go.

Then one day I realized I wasn't protecting the company anymore. I was protecting my ego. The past had done its job—it had taught me, refined me, rewarded me. But it was time to pivot again.

When I finally let go, I didn't lose my story. I expanded it. That's the paradox of the sunk-cost trap: you think you're abandoning your past, but really, you're honoring it by applying its lessons to something new.

Reflection Exercise: The Sunk-Cost Cleanse

Grab your journal and answer the following honestly:

What area of my life feels too expensive to leave? What am I afraid of losing if I do? What have I already lost by staying? If I were starting fresh today, knowing what I know now, would I choose this again? What would freedom look like if I gave myself permission to leave?

Then write this at the bottom of the page: "I honor my past by not chaining myself to it." Read it every day for a week. Watch how the emotional weight begins to lift.

Closing Thought

You don't owe your future to the time, money, or effort you've already spent. You owe it to the person you're still becoming.

Everything you've done so far has brought you here—to the edge of clarity. Now it's time to decide: will you keep paying rent to your past? Or will you invest in your future?

Your past was the down payment. Your future is the home.

Chapter Seven

Fear Mapping & Risk Budgeting

Turning Fear Into a Framework

"Fear unexamined is paralysis. Fear defined is data."

The Fog of Fear

Fear is powerful not because it's big, but because it's blurry.

We say things like: I'm scared to leave my job. What if I fail? What if this doesn't work out? But if you stop and ask, What exactly am I afraid of? most people can't answer clearly.

Fear thrives in vagueness. It feeds on fog. The moment you define it—the moment you shine light on its edges—fear begins to shrink. That's not poetic; it's biological. The human brain treats uncertainty as danger. When you don't know what might happen, your nervous system assumes everything bad could happen. That's why vague fear feels like drowning—you can't grab hold of anything.

So the goal isn't to eliminate fear. The goal is to map it—to give it shape, size, and scale. Once you can see it, you can manage it.

"Clarity is the cure for fear."

The Biology of Fear

When you perceive a threat—physical, emotional, or financial—your amygdala, the brain's alarm center, fires like a smoke detector. It doesn't care whether the fire is real or imagined; it just wants you safe.

But here's the catch: your brain can't distinguish between a lion chasing you and a new career decision. It triggers the same physiological response: racing heart, shallow breath, adrenaline, cortisol. You think you're in danger, when really you're just stepping into the unknown.

This is why fear feels physical—because it is. But once you label it, once you engage your prefrontal cortex—the reasoning brain—the alarm quiets. That's what fear mapping does: it moves fear from your body to your brain, from emotion to analysis.

Fear Mapping: Making the Invisible Visible

Start with a sentence that captures your hesitation: I'm afraid to leave my job. I'm scared to start my business. I'm nervous to end this relationship.

Now ask yourself: What am I really afraid of? List every possible answer—no matter how small, silly, or catastrophic it sounds. If you're afraid to leave a job, your list might include: What if I run out of money? What if no one hires me again? What if I fail and people think I'm foolish? What if I can't handle the stress? What if it's worse somewhere else?

Once the list is out, something shifts. Your brain starts to relax. Why? Because uncertainty just became information. Now we can work with it.

Step 1: Probability

Ask: How likely is this, really? Will you truly never get hired again? Will you run out of money forever? Will everyone judge you?

When you force fears into measurable probabilities, they stop being infinite. Rate each fear on a scale of 1 to 10, with 1 being very unlikely and 10 being very likely.

Step 2: Reversibility

Next, ask: If this did happen, how reversible is it? Could you get another job? Freelance for income? Rebuild savings within a year? Move in with family temporarily?

You'll realize most fears are reversible, not permanent. The few that aren't—threats to health, safety, or integrity—are the ones truly worth designing around.

Step 3: Mitigation

For each fear, write one possible antidote. Fear of running out of money? Build a three-month emergency fund before you pivot. Fear of failing publicly? Document your journey honestly rather than performing results. Fear of losing confidence? Work with a mentor weekly. Fear of burning bridges? Leave with professionalism and genuine gratitude.

When you finish, the page that once felt terrifying looks tactical. Fear has lost its mystery. It's not a monster—it's math.

"Once you put fear on paper, it stops living rent-free in your head."

The Illusion of Safety

Many people think the safest choice is the familiar one —staying in the same job, the same environment, the same identity.

But staying carries its own risks that most people never calculate. Staying in an unfulfilling job risks burnout, resentment, and emotional erosion. Staying in a toxic relationship risks lost self-worth and missed joy. Staying quiet about your dreams risks lifelong regret.

When you start budgeting risk instead of fearing it, you realize every option has a cost. The question isn't Is this risky? It's Which risk am I willing to take?

Risk Budgeting: The Currency of Courage

Think of your risk tolerance like a financial budget. You have a finite amount of emotional, mental, and financial energy. The key isn't to avoid spending it—it's to spend wisely.

Imagine allocating 100 risk points across your life decisions. Leaving a job might cost 40 points—worth it to align with purpose and reclaim time. Starting a business might cost 25—worth it to build long-term autonomy. Moving cities might cost 20—worth it to expand your network and inspiration. Ending an unfulfilling relationship might cost 15—worth it to rebuild emotional safety.

Now ask: Am I over-spending on the wrong risks? Staying in burnout (emotional risk) might be costing you far more than starting fresh (financial risk). Avoiding rejection (social risk) might be costing more than trying and failing (growth risk). When you visualize risk this way, fear transforms from an enemy into an investment strategy.

"You can't eliminate risk—you can only reallocate it."

A Story of Fear Turned Fuel

Years ago, I met a future founder who wanted to leave his comfortable role at Goldman Sachs to build his own company. He had the skills, the savings, and a plan—but he couldn't move.

"I'm just scared," he told me. "What if it fails?"

So I asked him to define failure. He said going broke. I asked how long until he'd hit zero. He calculated: maybe a year. Could he freelance if it got tight? Yes. Move somewhere cheaper? Yes. Return to corporate if he needed to? Easily.

We both laughed. What had felt like a bottomless pit suddenly had a floor. Six months later he launched. A few years after that, he sold the company—then built and sold a few more. He'd long since replaced his old salary and gained something far rarer: peace, fulfillment, and the confidence that came from having answered his own "What if?" He now helps others do the same.

He didn't conquer fear by ignoring it. He conquered it by defining it.

The Real Risk: Regret

In every pivot, there's one fear that overshadows all the rest: regret.

Regret is the cost of not trying—the quiet ache that grows louder with time. Psychologists who study people near the end of their lives find one consistent theme: their biggest regret isn't having failed. It's having never tried.

You can bounce back from rejection. You can learn from failure. You can even laugh at embarrassment years later. But you can't recover from wondering what might have been.

What if you had written the book? Started the company? Walked away from what was draining you? Every time you ignore that call, regret compounds—and one day you look back and realize the greatest loss wasn't security or status. It was possibility.

When you put your fears on one side of the scale and regret on the other, regret always weighs more. The greatest risk is staying where your soul no longer fits.

Don't wait until life forces your hand. Listen now, while you still have time to answer your own "What if?" with courage instead of regret.

A Personal Moment: When Fear Almost Won

Before I left corporate life to start my own venture, I spent months frozen.

I had the plan, the skills, the resources. But fear kept whispering: You're risking everything. You have a family. You have a mortgage. So I sat down and made a list—every single thing that could go wrong. Twenty items. Then, next to each one, I wrote the worst possible outcome.

Halfway through, I started laughing. Most of my catastrophes were reversible. The rest were manageable. And one—the fear of never knowing what could have been—was unbearable.

I mapped it all out, gave myself six months to generate income, and accepted that the absolute worst case was selling the house and moving in temporarily with family. Then I took the leap. Fear wasn't my enemy. It was my teacher. Once I mapped it, I moved. And the moment I moved, momentum took over.

The Power of Micro-Bravery

You don't need to be fearless to pivot. You just need to be fractionally braver than your fear for ten seconds at a time.

Every act of courage has the same anatomy: **hesitation → decision → action → relief**. Start with small, low-risk experiments. Send one email to a potential mentor. Post one idea publicly. Have one honest conversation. Take one small step toward your pivot.

Each act builds your bravery muscle. Courage compounds.

"Bravery isn't the absence of fear. It's the accurate reading of it."

Reflection Exercise: Your Fear Map

Take fifteen quiet minutes. Open your notebook and write: What change or decision am I most afraid of right now?

List every fear connected to it—no censoring. For each, ask: How likely is this? How reversible is this? What could I do to prevent or recover from it?

Circle the one fear that feels most potent, then take one micro-action against it this week. Fear shrinks in proportion to movement.

Closing Thought

Fear will never disappear. It's wired into you for survival. But survival isn't the same as success.

The goal isn't to be fearless—it's to be fear-literate. When you can name, rate, and budget your fears, they stop running your life and start refining your plan.

So the next time fear whispers, What if it doesn't work? whisper back: What if it does? Then map it, budget it, and move forward anyway.

Courage isn't the absence of fear. It's the decision to move with it, not for it.

Chapter Eight

The Pivot Mindset

You Are Not What You Do—You Are What You Can Become

"You're not defined by your title. You're defined by your ability to evolve."

The Trap of Titles

Ask someone, Who are you? Chances are they'll answer with their job title.

I'm a lawyer. I'm an engineer. I'm a teacher. I'm just a mom.

Notice something? Those answers describe roles, not identities. Roles change. Identities evolve. But when we fuse the two, we build a fragile self-concept—one that collapses the moment life changes.

The Pivot Mindset begins when you realize: you are not your role. You are the energy behind it.

Labels as Shackles

Our culture loves labels because they make people predictable. But labels also make people limited.

You start to live inside invisible walls: I can't switch careers—I'm a finance person. I can't speak on stage—

I'm introverted. I can't start a business—I'm a mom. I can't slow down—I'm a CEO.

Each statement sounds responsible. But it's really a confession of captivity. Labels can feel comforting because they provide identity. Over time, though, they become handcuffs disguised as certainty. The moment you start saying I am only this, you close the door to who you could become.

"Labels make life simpler, not richer."

Identity Is a Story, Not a Sentence

Here's the secret few people realize: identity isn't fixed. It's narrated.

You are constantly telling a story about who you are —to others, but more importantly, to yourself. That story becomes your reality. If your story says I'm not creative, you'll unconsciously avoid creative opportunities. If it says I'm too old to change, you'll ignore signs that it's time to grow.

But if your story says I'm adaptable, I'm a lifelong learner, I evolve—then no setback or pivot can threaten you, because reinvention is built into your identity.

That's the Pivot Mindset: you are not the noun you've been called. You are the verb of becoming.

The Science of Self-Concept

Psychologists call this self-schema—the mental model of who we think we are. Our brains crave consistency, so they filter experience through that lens, ignoring anything that contradicts the story.

That's why change feels so threatening: it's not just about losing comfort; it's about losing identity. But here's the good news: the same brain that clings to identity is capable of rewriting it.

When you deliberately update your self-schema—from I'm bad with risk to I'm learning to make smart risks—your brain begins seeking evidence to support the new version. Identity follows intention. The shift happens not when you decide to believe something new, but when you act on it and see the results. Beliefs and behavior are in a continuous loop: each one reshapes the other. Permission to Pivot is designed to help you initiate that loop.

"Your brain works for the identity you assign it."

Stories of Reinvention

History is filled with people who smashed the mold and rewrote who they were.

Vera Wang didn't design her first dress until forty, after careers in journalism and competitive figure skating. Colonel Sanders launched KFC in his sixties after decades of setbacks. Martha Stewart moved from Wall Street to homemaking. Julia Child worked in intelligence before discovering cooking at thirty-six.

None of them had certainty. They had willingness. They weren't loyal to who they'd been—they were loyal to who they were becoming. That's the essence of the Pivot Mindset.

A Modern Example

A few years ago, I met a man named Rob who had been a dentist for twenty-two years. Respected, stressed, and miserable.

"I feel like I'm dying one patient at a time," he told me. When I asked what he'd do if money weren't a factor, he said he'd teach people how to build small businesses. He'd always loved entrepreneurship; he just never gave himself permission to claim it.

After months of reflection, he pivoted. Today he runs a thriving coaching practice helping other medical professionals escape burnout. He didn't throw away his past—he repurposed it. The precision, empathy, and leadership that made him a good dentist now makes him a phenomenal mentor. He didn't need a new identity. He needed a new application of the one he already had.

"Your past chapters aren't dead ends. They're raw material for what's next."

Identity Shift: From Role to Resource

When you strip away the titles, what's left? Not emptiness—essence.

You are not an accountant. You are analytical. You are not a teacher. You are communicative and empathetic. You are not an athlete. You are disciplined and driven. You are not just a parent. You are nurturing and resilient.

Your job title is the stage. Your character traits are the actors. And those actors can perform in any play.

The Cost of Fixed Identity

When you cling too tightly to one version of yourself, you start defending it even when it's outdated.

You become so busy proving who you were that you forget to grow into who you could be. That's how people stay in jobs, relationships, or habits long after they've expired—not because they're incapable of change, but because they're addicted to consistency. They'd rather be certainly miserable than possibly free.

Your identity isn't meant to be a fortress. It's meant to be a bridge. You can't cross to your next chapter while guarding the one behind you.

"If you cling to who you were, you'll never meet who you're meant to be."

The Fluid Self

The Pivot Mindset embraces identity as fluid, not fixed. Fluid identity doesn't mean you lack direction—it means you have range.

Think of water. It takes the shape of whatever container it occupies—a river, a bottle, a wave—but it's still water. You're the same. Your essence doesn't change; only your form does. When you adopt that belief, change no longer threatens you. It expresses you.

The Adaptive Advantage

Adaptability is the new intelligence. In a world where industries are disrupted, technologies replaced, and roles redefined faster than ever, the most valuable skill isn't mastery of a specific task—it's the ability to pivot gracefully.

Adaptability means you can learn faster than your environment changes. You can update your beliefs as you evolve. You can navigate uncertainty with curiosity instead of fear. That's not just resilience—it's reinvention.

"The most powerful identity you can hold is simply: I can adapt."

A Personal Reflection: My Identity Unraveled

When I sold my first company, I faced an identity crisis I didn't expect.

For years, entrepreneur was who I was. It wasn't just my job—it was my proof of worth. After the sale, people would ask, So what do you do now? And I didn't have an answer. I felt invisible, irrelevant, even lost.

Until I realized I wasn't the CEO of a company. I was the creator of possibility. That's who I'd always been. The company was just one expression of that.

Once I understood that, my creativity exploded. I started new ventures, wrote, invested, and mentored.

Because when you know your essence, you'll always find new expressions for it. You can take away the title. You can't erase the truth of who you are.

How to Practice the Pivot Mindset

Start with a language audit. Pay attention to the words you use to describe yourself. Every "I am" statement reinforces identity. Replace limiting ones—I'm not a leader, I'm not creative—with fluid ones: I'm developing leadership skills, I'm exploring creativity. Shift your vocabulary and your identity will follow.

Second, adopt a learner's posture. People who pivot easily aren't smarter—they're more willing to learn. Every new skill starts with awkwardness. Rebrand that discomfort as evidence of growth. Ask yourself weekly: What stretched me this week? Where did I feel resistance? What did that teach me about myself?

Third, borrow future identities. Ask: Who would I be if I were already living my next chapter? Then practice thinking, speaking, and behaving like that version today. You're not faking it—you're forecasting it.

Fourth, rewrite your bio. Take your professional summary and remove every title and company name. Rewrite it focused on your values and abilities. Instead of I'm a marketing director with ten years of experience, try: I help ideas grow by connecting strategy, story, and people. One describes a job. The other describes a calling.

Reflection Exercise: The Identity Inventory

Open your journal and write:

What titles or roles have I been defining myself by? Which of those no longer fit who I'm becoming? What qualities or values have remained constant through every chapter of my life?

Write five new "I am" statements that describe your essence, not your job. Then post one somewhere visible —your desk, your phone, your mirror—as a daily reminder: I am not my role. I am my evolution.

Closing Thought

Your degree, your title, your habits—they're chapters, not your whole book.

Every pivot begins when you stop asking, Who am I to do this? and start declaring, Who else would I rather be?

Your identity isn't your résumé. It's your ability to adapt, learn, and evolve.

So shed the labels. Rewrite the story. And remember: you're not defined by what you've done. You're defined by what you're still willing to become.

Chapter Nine

Crafting a Personal Pivot Thesis

Clarity Creates Courage

"When your why is clear, the how finds its way."

The Power of Clarity

Most people don't stay stuck because they lack talent or opportunity. They stay stuck because they lack clarity.

They feel the urge to change—the pull toward something more aligned—but it's just a fog. A vague ache that whispers, This isn't it. And so they do what most of us do when we don't have clarity: they wait.

But clarity doesn't appear by waiting. It appears by writing. When you put your thoughts on paper, feelings become form. Ideas turn into architecture.

That's what this chapter is about: creating your Personal Pivot Thesis—a written statement that defines your why, your what, and your how. This is the blueprint for your next chapter. Not a wish, not a fantasy—a declaration.

"Until your pivot has language, it remains a feeling. Once you name it, it becomes a mission."

Why You Need a Pivot Thesis

Think of your pivot thesis as your north star—a clear, written compass that keeps you grounded when fear, doubt, or confusion start to swirl.

Without one, you drift. You second-guess yourself. You get pulled back by inertia or distracted by noise. With one, you have direction, criteria, and purpose. A pivot thesis doesn't lock you into a rigid plan—it gives your change a heartbeat, a reason to exist, and a way to measure success.

It answers the three questions every meaningful transformation must confront: Why now? What changes? What does success look like?

The Anatomy of a Pivot Thesis

Your thesis has three essential parts.

1. Why Now? (The Emotional Core)

Every pivot begins with a pulse—a sense that staying the same has become too costly. Maybe it's the boredom that won't leave, the dread that keeps growing, or the craving that's been calling your name for years.

Ask yourself: What has changed that makes inaction unbearable? What are the signals I can no longer ignore? What pain am I trying to end, or what possibility am I trying to reach? When you name your why, you give your pivot gravity. It's no longer an experiment—it's a necessity.

"The moment your reason becomes real, your excuses dissolve."

---

2. What Changes? (The Practical Shift)

Once you know why, define what. Be specific—vague pivots die in vague plans.

I'm leaving corporate finance to pursue entrepreneurship. I'm transitioning from management to teaching. I'm moving cities to prioritize a slower, healthier pace. I'm ending a relationship that no longer supports mutual growth.

You don't need to know every step—just the direction of movement. Think of this part as drawing the coordinates on your map: This is where I'm headed next.

3. Success Criteria (The Emotional ROI)

This element is crucial, and most people skip it. You need to define how you'll measure the success of your pivot—not by money, not by titles, but by alignment.

How do I want to feel every day? What kind of energy do I want to bring into my life? How will I know I made the right move?

When you define success by feeling, you prevent yourself from trading one misfit for another that just looks different.

"If you don't define success, the world will define it for you—and you'll end up back where you started."

The Power of Written Commitment

Writing your thesis is more than symbolic. It's neurological.

Studies show that writing by hand increases neural engagement and emotional commitment—converting abstract ideas into actionable memory. Your brain treats written words as instructions. So when you write your pivot thesis, you're not just describing a change. You're programming it.

It's no longer a wish in your head. It's a mission on paper. That single act separates dreamers from doers.

How to Write Your Pivot Thesis

Take a quiet hour. No phone, no scrolling, no distractions. Just you and a blank page.

Section One—Why Now: Write two to three sentences explaining what has changed and why this pivot matters now. Example: I've spent years in a career that no longer excites or challenges me. I feel a deep need to use my creativity and autonomy more fully. Staying here feels like betraying the next version of myself.

Section Two—What Changes: Write one clear sentence defining your pivot. Example: I am leaving corporate finance within the next six months to pursue entrepreneurship in a field that aligns with my strengths in communication and innovation.

Section Three—Success Criteria: List three measurable or emotional indicators of success. Example: I will know this pivot succeeded when I feel energized rather than depleted by my daily work, when I experience genuine autonomy over my time and decisions, and when I can see tangible impact from what I create.

Now combine your answers into a formal thesis. Read it aloud. If it makes you feel a mix of excitement and fear—good. That's the right one.

A Sample Pivot Thesis

"I am leaving corporate finance within the next six months to pursue entrepreneurship. My measure of success is building a business that aligns with my values of creativity, autonomy, and impact. My why now is the growing awareness that staying would mean sacrificing joy and purpose for comfort—a trade I'm no longer willing to make."

Simple. Powerful. Honest. This isn't a slogan—it's a declaration of intent. Once written, it becomes your contract with yourself.

The Accountability Effect

Once your pivot is written, tell someone you trust—a mentor, partner, or coach.

Saying it aloud activates accountability. It shifts your brain from internal wish to external expectation. Accountability isn't pressure—it's proof that you take your life seriously. You're not just talking about change. You're inviting support for it.

Evolving the Thesis Over Time

A pivot thesis isn't a contract carved in stone. It's a living document.

You'll refine it as you move—adjusting timelines, redefining success, deepening your why. Think of it like a GPS: you set your destination, but you're free to take detours, reroutes, and scenic roads. Update it quarterly. Revisit your why when doubt creeps in. Celebrate small wins as evidence that your thesis is unfolding in real time.

Common Mistakes to Avoid

Writing for others instead of yourself. The thesis is for your alignment, not your résumé. Don't write what sounds impressive—write what feels true.

Being too vague. "I want to be happier" is noble but useless. Define what happier looks like in daily life.

Skipping the why now. Without urgency, you'll procrastinate. Tie your pivot to something real and current.

Measuring only by outcome. You can't control timing or results—but you can control alignment and effort. Always include emotional success markers.

Hiding it away. Post your thesis somewhere visible. It's not decoration; it's direction.

A Personal Story: My Own Pivot Thesis

Years ago, before I took the leap into full-time entrepreneurship, I wrote my first pivot thesis on a yellow legal pad. It read:

> *"I am transitioning from selling someone else's vision to building my own. I've spent years creating growth and success for other companies—now it's time to do it for mine. My next chapter is about ownership, creativity, and impact. I'm done fueling someone else's dream. It's time to scale my own."*

At the time, it felt audacious. But it gave me structure. That one paragraph became my north star. Whenever fear crept in, I'd reread it. It reminded me why I was walking away from stability toward purpose.

When I eventually built my first company—and later, several more—I realized something profound: it wasn't the business plan that made it happen. It was the personal plan. Clarity creates courage, every single time.

Reflection Exercise: Write Your Personal Pivot Thesis

Set aside forty-five minutes and work through these three steps.

Step One—Why Now: What pain or restlessness pushed you to consider change? What signs are telling you this chapter is complete? What's at stake if you stay the same for another year? Five years?

Step Two—What Changes: What are you moving from and toward? What new possibilities excite you most? What small step could you take within the next thirty days?

Step Three—Success Criteria: What would fulfillment look like six months from now? What emotions will tell you you're on the right track? How will you celebrate progress, not just results?

Combine your answers into a three-to-five sentence paragraph. Then, at the bottom of the page, write this and sign it: "I give myself permission to outgrow what I've outlived."

Date it. Keep it. You're not promising to never feel fear or doubt—you're promising to stay honest, curious, and courageous enough to keep moving forward.

Closing Thought

Clarity doesn't remove fear. It replaces confusion with conviction.

Your Pivot Thesis is your compass—the document that reminds you where you're going and why it matters. When the old world calls you back with its comforts and habits, reread it. When uncertainty clouds your path, reread it. When you question whether you're cut out for this, reread it.

You wrote it in your clearest moment. It will guide you through your darkest.

This is the moment you stop drifting and start directing. This is where your pivot becomes a plan.

"The future belongs to those who write their own thesis."

Chapter Ten

Public vs. Private Permission

You Don't Need a Permission Slip to Live Your Life

"The moment you stop waiting for permission is the moment your life begins to expand."

The Great Permission Myth

If there's one invisible force that keeps most people from pivoting, it's not fear. It's permission.

They wait for it. They crave it. They subtly, sometimes subconsciously, seek it—from parents, peers, mentors, social media followers, from the invisible committee in their heads that votes on whether it's okay to change.

But here's the truth: nobody can authorize your evolution but you. The world won't hand you a hall pass for your own potential. You have to sign it yourself.

"Waiting for permission is the most polite form of self-sabotage."

Why We Seek Permission

It's not weakness—it's wiring.

From childhood, most of us are conditioned to look outward for validation. We raise our hands before we speak. We wait to be picked for teams. We look for grades, gold stars, promotions, likes. We learn that approval equals safety.

So when the time comes to pivot—to break the pattern, change paths, or pursue something new—our first instinct is to ask: Will they understand? Will they agree?

But here's the paradox: the people who love you most often have the hardest time accepting your change. They're not trying to hold you back; they're trying to keep you safe inside the identity they recognize. Your growth threatens their certainty. Your change challenges their comfort. So if you wait for everyone to cheer before you move, you'll wait forever.

"People can only meet you where they've met themselves."

Two Kinds of Permission

There are two paths to giving yourself permission to pivot.

Public permission means announcing your intentions, inviting accountability and support. Private permission means moving quietly first, protecting your pivot while it's still fragile. Neither is right or wrong. Both work—in different contexts.

Public Permission: Power in the Open

When you share your pivot out loud—with friends, colleagues, or your community—you gain accountability. Saying it transforms "I might" into "I will." You attract allies. Opportunities, introductions, and encouragement appear from unexpected places. The act of declaring creates psychological commitment.

The risks are real too: not everyone will understand, and announcing too early exposes your pivot to criticism before it's ready to stand. Some people feel obligated to deliver fast once they've gone public, even when the process needs patience. Public permission works best when you thrive on accountability, when your pivot requires visible support, and when you're mentally ready to defend your why.

Example: The Artist Who Went Public

I once worked with a client named Jenna—a marketing executive who wanted to become a full-time artist. She'd been painting for years in secret, hiding her work from colleagues. One day, she posted a single piece on LinkedIn: This is the side of me I've kept quiet. I'm finally giving it a voice.

Within twenty-four hours, old coworkers commissioned work and a friend offered a gallery connection. That one act of public permission shifted her trajectory. Because when you declare your pivot, you give others permission to evolve too.

Private Permission: Power in the Quiet

Private permission means moving first—quietly. You build traction before broadcasting. You give yourself space to grow before the world weighs in.

The advantages are focus, freedom to experiment privately, and the unshakeable confidence that comes from having results before an audience. The risks are isolation and the fear loop that can develop without accountability. Perfectionism is the other trap—waiting until everything feels ready, which may never come. Private permission works best when your pivot is emotionally sensitive, when you're still building clarity, or when outside opinions could derail your focus.

Example: The Engineer Who Moved in Silence

A software engineer named Luis dreamed of opening a surf school in Costa Rica, but every time he mentioned it, people laughed. So he stopped talking and started planning. He researched markets, identified partners, built a website, and saved aggressively for eighteen months. When he finally announced it, it wasn't a dream—it was a launch. Sometimes, silence isn't fear. It's strategy.

> *"Sometimes the most powerful permission slip is the one nobody sees."*

A Personal Example: Moving Without Permission

I had a vision to build a business that would solve a problem I saw inside a large college system: agencies controlled the data, hid performance, and raised prices —black-box marketing with no transparency. I pitched it internally. It was ignored.

At home, my wife and in-laws were terrified I'd leave a stable job to chase it. The pressure came fast: This is reckless. Think of your family. Don't do it. I had zero external permission and plenty of pressure not to move.

But the inner voice wouldn't quit. So I issued private permission to myself, mapped the model, built quietly, and took the first steps without an audience. That idea became CUnet—and went from concept to acquisition in under two and a half years. I didn't have permission. I had conviction. And that was enough.

The Danger of Waiting for Validation

Here's where most people get stuck: they confuse permission with validation. They think, Once people support me, then I'll move. But validation is conditional. Permission is internal.

If your desire for change depends on applause, your growth will always be at the mercy of other people's comfort zones. You'll spend your life editing yourself for audiences that were never meant to understand you. The truth is, you don't need validation to move forward. You need alignment. The people who truly matter will catch up later—once they see you thriving.

"You can't build a new life from someone else's approval."

The Private-First Strategy

If you're unsure which path to take, consider a hybrid approach: start private for thirty to ninety days. Build quietly. Get small wins. Then, once you have traction and confidence, share selectively with people who can support or accelerate your progress. Let your actions become your announcement.

Managing Criticism and Doubt

No matter how thoughtfully you pivot, someone will question it. Criticism often mirrors the critic's fear, not your flaw. When people say, I could never do that, what they often mean is, I'm scared you're proving I could. So instead of defending your decision, simply say, I understand—and move forward. You don't owe anyone an explanation for your evolution.

The "If Nobody Clapped" Test

Ask yourself: If nobody clapped or criticized, would I still want this pivot? If the answer is yes, you've found truth. If the answer is no, you've found performance. Because a life worth living doesn't require an audience.

Reflection Exercise: Building Your Internal Approval System

Take ten minutes and answer honestly: Who have I been unconsciously waiting to approve my pivot? What am I afraid will happen if they don't? What evidence do I already have that I can trust myself? What would change if I gave myself permission to proceed today?

Then write your private permission slip: "I hereby give myself permission to evolve without explanation, without applause, and without apology." Sign it. Date it. Keep it. You don't need consensus. You need conviction.

Closing Thought

Public or private—your pivot is valid. Some journeys thrive in the spotlight. Others bloom in silence. What matters isn't how loud your change is—it's how true it is.

You don't need applause to evolve. You don't need understanding to begin. Start small. Start quietly. Start anyway.

Because the most powerful permission slip in the world isn't signed by your boss, your partner, or your peers. It's signed by you.

"The day you stop asking for permission is the day your life becomes yours again."

Part Three

Move

Design & Execute Your Pivot Plan

Awareness and decision mean nothing without action. Part III is about movement—turning your insights and permission into forward progress. Pivots don't require reckless leaps. They require designed steps.

This section provides the practical playbook: running low-risk experiments, creating milestones, assembling your support system, rewiring habits, planning your finances, communicating your decision with confidence, and surviving the inevitable dip when enthusiasm wanes.

Chapters in Part Three

CHAPTER ELEVEN

Tiny Experiments, Big Clarity

How Small Tests Create Massive Momentum

> *"You don't need to leap off a cliff to change your life. You just need to take one honest step that gives you new information—and forward momentum."*

The Myth of the Leap

When people imagine reinvention, they often picture something dramatic—quitting the job, ending the relationship, selling everything, moving abroad. Hollywood loves the leap. Social media glamorizes it. But in real life, the leap is usually unnecessary and sometimes reckless.

You don't have to risk everything to change everything. Most meaningful pivots begin not with a leap, but with an experiment—small, intentional tests done quietly and consistently that generate clarity without catastrophe.

> *"Big lives are built on small experiments."*

Why Experiments Work

Here's the problem with daydreams: they're too clean. From a distance, every new life looks perfect. The chef never deals with burnout. The writer never faces deadlines. The entrepreneur never worries about cash flow. But reality is different. Every dream has a texture—a rhythm, a daily grind that you can't see from afar.

Experiments collapse that fantasy into feedback. They let you try before you buy. You gather data instead of daydreams. You feel the truth of a new path before you stake your whole future on it.

The Power of Prototyping

Designers don't build final products on day one. They build prototypes—testing, tweaking, and observing before committing. You can do the same with your life.

A pivot prototype is a small, low-risk test that answers one question: Do I actually want this? Before you move across the country, spend a month there. Before you start a business, do one freelance project. Before you switch careers, shadow someone already doing it. You're not chickening out—you're collecting data.

"Every experiment is a vote for your next version."

Three Kinds of Tiny Experiments

1. Side Gigs: Testing the Work

A side gig is the single best way to prototype a new career without burning bridges. It's a sandbox—a safe space to experiment and see if the excitement lasts once fantasy meets friction.

If you're curious about coaching, offer three free sessions to friends and track your energy during and after. If you want to write, commit to publishing one article a week for a month. If you dream of real estate, shadow an agent on weekends. If you want to start an e-commerce business, sell a few products on Etsy or eBay first. The goal is to test real-world interest and discover whether the process excites you as much as the idea.

"Your side gig is not a distraction—it's your laboratory."

2. Informational Interviews: Testing the World

Sometimes the fastest way to clarity is through conversation, not action. An informational interview isn't a job pitch—it's a learning mission. You're gathering intelligence from people who live the life you're considering.

Ask: What surprised you most about this path? What do you wish you'd known before starting? What does a typical day look like? Commit to five conversations with people in your new field. By the end, patterns will emerge. You'll see what's fantasy and what's fact—and you'll often find allies willing to open doors.

"Clarity compounds through curiosity."

3. Thirty-Day Challenges: Testing Yourself

The best experiments don't test the external world—they test your internal consistency. A thirty-day challenge is a focused experiment to build new habits and test your own follow-through.

Write for thirty minutes a day. Exercise every morning for a month. Code, paint, or meditate daily. Wake up an hour earlier to work on your idea. Thirty days is long enough to see patterns, short enough to stay doable. By the end, you'll know: Do I actually enjoy this? Does it give me energy or drain it? Can I imagine doing this long-term?

"Short experiments reveal lifelong truths."

Case Study: The Weekend Entrepreneur

When Sarah told me she wanted to leave her finance job to start a bakery, I didn't tell her to quit. I told her to bake. "Run a thirty-day test," I said. "Sell cupcakes every weekend for a month. Track your energy, profits, and excitement."

Week one, she loved the creativity but was overwhelmed by logistics. Week two, she streamlined her process and found joy in customer interactions. Week three, she started selling out. Week four, she realized she didn't want to run a bakery—she wanted to teach baking. That's the beauty of experiments. They don't just confirm your desires—they refine them. Sarah didn't fail. She found truth faster.

"Every small test eliminates one wrong road and lights the right one."

How to Design a Great Experiment

A good experiment has four ingredients: low risk (you shouldn't lose your savings if it doesn't pan out), short duration (seven to thirty days), a clear hypothesis (If I do X, I'll learn Y), and a trackable outcome—something you can measure, even if that measurement is emotional.

Here's a quick example. Goal: explore whether wellness coaching is right for you. Hypothesis: If I take on three clients for free, I'll learn whether coaching energizes me. Duration: thirty days. Metrics: client feedback, my own energy after sessions, desire to keep going. At the end, reflect: Did this feed me or drain me? If it feeds you, expand. If it drains you, refine. Either way, you win—because you have data, not doubt.

Why Tiny Works Better Than Huge

Big changes trigger big fear. Your brain's job is survival, not success—it interprets radical change as danger. But small steps? Your nervous system can handle that.

Tiny experiments create psychological safety. They tell your brain: We're exploring, not exploding. That's why small wins compound so powerfully—they bypass resistance while still building proof. Each experiment becomes evidence that you can learn, adapt, and move without losing everything.

"Small wins are the scaffolding of big change."

The Emotional Side of Experimenting

Experiments teach more than skill—they teach self-trust. Each test builds what psychologists call agency: the belief that you can affect your own life through action. Most people lose that belief because they've been trained to overanalyze and under-act.

Once you see yourself take one small action and survive—maybe even thrive—your self-trust returns. And with it, momentum. That's how pivots begin: not with certainty, but with evidence of capability.

"Confidence isn't only built by thinking you can. It's built by proving you can."

Case Study: Mike—From Business Development to Global Wellness Leader

Mike worked with me at several of my companies over the years—sharp, magnetic, full of humor and heart. He'd started in sales, moved into business development, and was genuinely excellent at both.

So when he told me he was leaving to become a personal trainer, my honest reaction was: Are you kidding me? He followed through anyway, got certified, and began training clients. He was serious and searching for something deeper—a career aligned with his passion for health and human performance. The transition wasn't seamless; the day-to-day of being an independent trainer didn't fully satisfy his need for growth. Eventually, he returned to the business world, and I welcomed him back without hesitation.

But the story didn't end there. A year later, Mike left again—this time landing a role leading wellness initiatives for a fast-growing global technology company. Over the following years, he traveled the world opening gyms and corporate wellness programs across continents. Today, he's the global head of wellness for that organization, building healthier cultures at scale.

Mike's journey is what this book stands for. He was excellent at what he did, but brave enough to admit something was missing. He tested his interests, discovered what didn't fit, and refined what did. When the first version of his pivot didn't land perfectly, he adjusted. Each step gave him clarity until he built a life that fused his professional skills with his personal passion. He didn't just switch jobs. He redesigned his purpose.

Reflection: Your First Thirty-Day Experiment

Take five minutes and design one. Choose a focus—what area needs testing? Define a small daily or weekly action. Set a hypothesis: what do you hope to learn? Schedule it. After thirty days, write down what surprised you.

No giant leap. Just data, clarity, and momentum.

Closing Thought

You don't have to have it all figured out before you move. You just have to run your next experiment. Each test—no matter how small—teaches you more about who you are and what you want.

Clarity doesn't come from certainty. It comes from curiosity, courage, and consistent testing. So start your experiment. Make it small. Make it simple. Make it real. You don't need a parachute leap. You just need a thirty-day test of faith.

Chapter Twelve

Milestone Mapping

Turning Overwhelming Leaps into Manageable Steps

> *"You don't climb a mountain by staring at the summit. You climb it by finding the next foothold."*

From Dream to Direction

Big pivots look exciting from afar, but up close they can feel impossible. When you're standing at the bottom of your next chapter—staring at a mountain of unknowns—your brain doesn't see opportunity. It sees danger. That's why most people freeze.

The solution is to break the mountain into milestones: concrete, measurable, achievable checkpoints that transform fear into focus. When you know your next three steps, you stop spinning in "someday" and start moving today.

> *"You don't need the full map. You just need the next mile marker."*

Why Milestones Matter

Without milestones, pivots feel like chaos. You're running on emotion instead of execution. Emotion is what starts the journey. Milestones are what sustain it. They provide structure, visibility, and momentum. Each small win generates the confidence to keep going.

> *"Progress you can see becomes progress you believe in."*

The Milestone Framework

Every successful pivot follows a sequence of checkpoints between where you are and where you want to be. Think of them as your GPS—each checkpoint gives you feedback, confidence, and a moment to recalibrate.

Start by defining your start point honestly. Then define your end point: where do you want to arrive in six to twelve months? From there, identify three to five milestones. Milestone One is the first clear sign of traction. Milestone Two is the first proof of concept. Milestone Three is the stabilization phase, where the new direction starts to feel sustainable.

Here's an example for a career pivot to freelancing. Start: current corporate role, feeling stagnant. Milestone One: build a portfolio—three client samples completed. Milestone Two: land a first paying client. Milestone Three: replace twenty-five percent of income with consistent projects. Milestone Four: financial runway in place, recurring clients established. End point: sustainable freelance business with freedom, alignment, and steady revenue. By dividing the dream into measurable checkpoints, you stop asking, How do I reinvent everything? and start asking, What's the next milestone? That question is answerable. And answerable means actionable.

Create KPIs for Life

In business, Key Performance Indicators track health, growth, and success. Your pivot deserves the same—and life KPIs don't have to be financial. They can measure progress in energy, learning, or alignment.

A career pivot might track three completed projects in a new industry. A financial pivot: debt reduced by a specific amount. A health pivot: consistent thirty-minute movement five times per week. A mindset pivot: daily journaling twenty days out of the month. The key is measurability. If you can't measure it, you can't track it. If you can't track it, you can't celebrate it.

"Vague goals create vague results.
Measurable goals create momentum."

The Emotional KPI

Not all KPIs are numeric. Some are felt. I wake up with curiosity instead of dread. I feel energized more days than exhausted. I feel proud when I describe what I do. Those count. In fact, they often matter most. Because the ultimate measure of a successful pivot isn't metrics—it's meaning.

Build Exit Ramps

Every milestone plan needs exit ramps—decision points where you pause, review, and decide whether to continue, pivot again, or change tactics. An exit ramp isn't failure. It's flexibility.

At the end of each milestone, ask: What's working better than expected? What's not working at all? Do I still want this goal? Is there a smarter, simpler route forward? Consider the startup founder who planned to raise capital in six months. After three months of pitching, investors aren't resonating—but customers are. That's an exit ramp moment. Plans aren't meant to be obeyed blindly. They're meant to be interrogated intelligently.

"Agility is not quitting. It's the art of continuing in the right direction."

Visualize Progress

The human brain is motivated not by perfection, but by progress it can see. Use a whiteboard, journal, or digital app. Draw your milestones along a simple horizontal line and check them off as you go. Track momentum in streaks. At the end of each week, score your energy on a scale of one to ten.

Progress is psychological currency. When you see it, you believe in it—and belief fuels consistency.

Case Study: The 1% Pivot

After years in a draining sales job, Marcus wanted to transition into fitness coaching. He couldn't afford to quit immediately. So we built a milestone map. Milestone One: get one paying client. Milestone Two: earn one thousand dollars per month part-time. Milestone Three: save six months of living expenses. Milestone Four: resign from the corporate role. Milestone Five: replace previous income with coaching revenue.

Each step felt small enough to manage yet big enough to matter. Two years later, he'd done it. The magic wasn't in the leap. It was in the layout.

"Clarity without checkpoints is chaos."

The 90-Day Rule

Most people overestimate what they can do in a week and underestimate what they can do in ninety days. Milestone mapping works best in quarterly sprints.

Choose a single domain. Define one major milestone for the next ninety days. Break it into three thirty-day mini-goals. Review progress at each thirty-day mark and adjust. Here's a financial example: ninety-day goal—pay off three thousand dollars in debt. Month one: audit expenses and cut five hundred dollars monthly. Month two: launch a side income stream. Month three: apply all extra income toward the debt. Celebrate at the end. Then set the next sprint. Stack enough sprints and your pivot compounds.

"Momentum is built in quarters, not minutes."

Celebrate Micro-Wins

Milestones aren't just for measurement—they're for celebration. Each checkpoint you hit deserves acknowledgment. When you celebrate, you reinforce progress. You tell your subconscious: This is working. Keep going.

Celebration doesn't have to be extravagant—write the win in a journal, take a day off, share the progress with a friend. What matters is pausing long enough to feel the success before rushing to the next thing. Because burnout doesn't come from doing too much—it comes from celebrating too little.

"Every small victory is a message to your brain: you are becoming who you said you would be."

Reflection Exercise: Your Milestone Map

Take twenty minutes and build your own. Define your destination. Identify three to five milestones that would signal progress. Define KPIs—what metrics or emotions will prove you're on track? Add exit ramps. Create a physical or digital tracker. Then review it weekly—not as a critic, but as a coach.

Closing Thought

Your pivot isn't a cliff to jump off—it's a staircase to climb. Each milestone is a step. Each step brings you closer. Progress isn't a feeling; it's a structure.

Stop trying to figure out the entire future. Just build your next milestone—and then the next. Because one day, you'll look up from the climb and realize you didn't just reach the summit. You built the path that got you there.

Chapter Thirteen

Building Your Pivot Crew

No One Pivots Alone

> *"If you want to go fast, go alone. If you want to go far, build a crew."*

The Myth of the Lone Pivot

We glorify the lone hero—the entrepreneur who bootstrapped in isolation, the visionary who defied the odds alone. It makes for a great story. But in real life, it's a lie. No one transforms in isolation.

Every successful pivot—whether in career, health, love, or life—happens inside a network of influence, encouragement, and accountability. Because reinvention is hard. You'll doubt yourself. You'll hit walls. You'll need perspective, reassurance, and sometimes a firm push forward. That's why you need a Pivot Crew.

The Three Core Roles of a Pivot Crew

1. Mentors: Borrowed Wisdom

A mentor is someone who's already walked a version of your path and is willing to shorten your learning curve. Mentors are time machines—they let you skip mistakes they've already made. They don't give you the answers; they give you insight.

Look for alignment, not fame. Seek authenticity, not hierarchy. A great mentor tells you the truth, not just what you want to hear. Remember reciprocity: bring value to them too. Ask them: What do you wish you'd done differently? What beliefs did you have to let go of to grow? What would you do if you were me, starting fresh today?

"A mentor is someone who sees your potential long before you do."

---

2. Peers: Shared Struggle, Shared Strength

Peers are the unsung heroes of every transformation—the friends, colleagues, or fellow travelers who are also in motion. They normalize uncertainty. They turn loneliness into community.

When you surround yourself with others chasing growth, you stop feeling strange for wanting more. They provide emotional safety, accountability, and perspective. Find them through mastermind groups, professional circles, or by forming a small pivot pod—three to five people who meet biweekly to share wins, challenges, and next steps.

"Iron sharpens iron—and accountability sharpens action."

---

3. Professionals: Structure, Objectivity, and Strategy

Sometimes you need more than encouragement. You need expert guidance. Coaches offer clarity and execution support. Therapists help with emotional processing. Consultants bring technical expertise. They offer structure when life feels chaotic, help separate emotion from strategy, and hold you accountable to your own goals.

Hiring support isn't weakness. It's wisdom. Even Olympic athletes have coaches—not because they're incapable, but because they're serious.

"Guidance isn't dependence. It's leverage."

Filtering Your Circle

Not everyone deserves a front-row seat to your reinvention. Some people drain energy. Some project their fears. Some try to keep you small because your growth challenges their comfort.

Do a circle audit. List your ten closest influences. Next to each name, write honestly: Drains or Charges. After each interaction, do you feel lighter or heavier? Act accordingly—spend more time with chargers, set boundaries with drainers. You don't have to cut everyone off. You curate access.

"You can love people and still outgrow their influence."

The Psychology of Social Energy

Neuroscience shows that emotions are contagious. Spending time around pessimistic or fearful people literally changes your brain chemistry—raising cortisol and lowering dopamine. Your energy adapts to the dominant frequency of your circle. Surround yourself with growth-minded people, and your nervous system learns to see possibility instead of threat.

Case Study: The Multi-Domain Pivot

When Jason decided to turn his life around at forty-two, he didn't just change careers—he changed everything. Out of shape, financially stressed, emotionally burnt out.

Instead of going it alone, he built a crew. A career coach for professional direction. A gym buddy for physical accountability. A therapist for emotional clarity. Two friends who met him weekly for breakfast to check in. Within a year, he'd lost forty pounds, started a business, and restored his marriage. His secret wasn't discipline. It was design.

"Discipline is great. Design is better."

Your Pivot Board

Think of this as building a Board of Advisors for your life. The roles you're looking to fill: a mentor five to ten years ahead of you for strategic guidance; a peer for accountability and shared growth; a coach or therapist for structure and perspective; a cheerleader for emotional encouragement; and a challenger—someone honest and direct—to keep you grounded.

You don't need them all at once. But having two or three of these roles filled changes everything. When you pivot alone, every obstacle feels like a crisis. When you pivot with a crew, every obstacle becomes a conversation.

How to Ask for Help

One of the hardest parts of building a crew is asking. We've been taught that independence is strength—that needing others is weakness. But the opposite is true.

When you reach out, frame it as an invitation, not a favor: "I'm in the middle of a big life transition, and I really admire how you've navigated change. Could I buy you coffee and pick your brain?" Most people love to help. They just need to be asked clearly and sincerely.

When the Old Crew Doesn't Come Along

Sometimes the hardest part of growth isn't building new relationships—it's outgrowing old ones. You'll change. They might not. And that's okay.

Some people were meant for your previous chapter, not your next. Don't resent them. Release with gratitude. Holding onto old dynamics out of loyalty is like trying to carry your past into your future—and there's no room for both.

"You can't step into your next level surrounded by people committed to your last one."

Reflection Exercise: Your Crew Map

Grab a notebook. Draw a circle with your name in the center. Draw three rings: inner circle (the three to five people you trust deeply), middle circle (the five to ten you engage with regularly), outer circle (the wider network, acquaintances, potential mentors).

Ask yourself: Who energizes me most? Who could I learn from next? Who do I need to limit exposure to? Before letting anyone influence your pivot, run the energy filter: Do they expand me or contract me? Do they have what I want emotionally—peace, integrity, purpose, joy? Do they genuinely want to see me win?

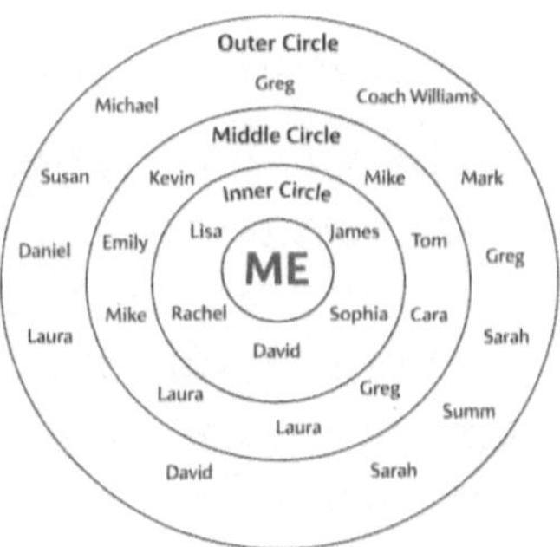

Closing Thought

You were never meant to pivot alone. Every meaningful change needs witnesses. Every bold step needs believers. Every great life needs a crew.

So build yours—intentionally, selectively, gratefully. Because the right people won't just support your pivot. They'll accelerate it.

"A strong crew turns your pivot from lonely to supported, from uncertain to strategic."

Chapter Fourteen

Habit Surgery

Cut What Kills. Build What Fuels.

"Big pivots don't fail because of big moves. They fail because of small, daily habits left unchecked."

The Real Reason Most Pivots Fail

Most pivots don't fail because of external barriers. They fail because the internal systems stay the same. You can change your job, your partner, your address—but if you wake up with the same thoughts, the same routines, and the same triggers, you'll recreate the same reality in a new setting.

That's why pivots are less about reinvention and more about reconstruction. Welcome to Habit Surgery—the precise, deliberate act of cutting what drains you and building what strengthens you.

"You can't build a new life with old habits."

Habits: The Invisible Architecture of Your Life

Think of habits as the operating system running beneath your daily consciousness. Every morning routine, every late-night scroll, every conversation pattern—they're lines of code that determine how you operate and what your life produces.

If your results aren't changing, it's because your code hasn't been rewritten. While willpower gets you started, habits keep you moving when motivation fades. And it will fade—especially in the messy middle of a pivot.

Step 1: Identify Your Keystone Habits

Charles Duhigg, author of The Power of Habit, coined the term "keystone habits"—habits that trigger a cascade of other positive behaviors. Like dominoes: push one, and several others fall in the right direction automatically.

Common keystone habits include exercise (which builds discipline, energy, and emotional regulation), journaling (which clears mental clutter), consistent sleep (which improves mood and resilience), morning planning (which creates intention), daily learning, and a gratitude practice. You don't need all of them—you just need one or two practiced consistently. A single commitment to morning exercise can cascade into earlier sleep, better nutrition, improved stress management, and a more confident start to every day.

"You don't rise to the level of your goals—
you fall to the level of your habits." —
James Clear

Step 2: Spot the Saboteurs

Not all habits build momentum. Some bleed it dry. Common saboteur habits include mindless scrolling that kills focus, drinking to escape stress, skipping sleep in the name of productivity, toxic conversations and gossip, starting the day with news and email before setting any intention, and constant multitasking.

Each one steals from the same account: your energy budget. During a pivot, energy is everything. You can't make courageous decisions with a depleted mind.

Step 3: The Surgery Process

Habit Surgery is a three-step process. First, identify the keystone habit to add. Second, identify the sabotaging habit to cut. Third, replace one with the other.

Behavior change sticks when you swap, not subtract. You don't break a bad habit by eliminating it—you replace it with a better one that meets the same emotional need in a healthier way. Replace late-night scrolling with reading before bed. Replace stress drinking with an evening walk. Replace checking email first thing with morning intention-setting. Replace complaining with a gratitude log. When you design replacements instead of restrictions, change becomes sustainable.

"The brain hates emptiness. If you remove a habit, you must replace it—or it will refill the void with something worse."

The Identity Connection

Every habit you reinforce tells your subconscious who you are. When you start saying, I'm the kind of person who plans my day, I'm the kind of person who moves my body, I'm the kind of person who protects my peace —your brain listens. You don't fake it until you make it. You repeat it until you become it.

The Habit Loop

Every habit follows the same neurological pattern: a cue triggers the behavior (the routine), and the reward is the payoff that keeps you doing it. To perform Habit Surgery effectively, dissect the loop. What triggers this habit? What reward am I really seeking? What alternative routine could satisfy that same reward in a better way?

Breaking the doomscroll loop as an example: Cue—feeling bored or anxious. Routine—grab the phone, scroll social media. Reward—momentary distraction. Surgery plan: put your phone in another room (change the cue); when anxious, take a short walk (change the routine); keep the reward—relaxation—but earn it through movement. Awareness, substitution, repetition. That's how you reprogram behavior.

Keystone Habits That Power Every Pivot

A morning grounding practice of just twenty minutes can change everything: five minutes of movement, five of journaling or intention-setting, five of silence or gratitude, five reviewing your top three priorities. Skip the chaos. Start with clarity.

A nighttime shutdown matters equally: no screens thirty minutes before bed, a brief reflection on what worked and what you learned, a consistent bedtime. Sleep is your pivot's silent superpower—everything else collapses without it.

Daily movement boosts dopamine, serotonin, and BDNF—the protein linked to cognitive growth. When you move, you think better. When you think better, you decide better. And pivots are just a series of better decisions. Input management matters too: unfollow accounts that drain your peace, replace doomscrolling with learning content. Every scroll is a vote for your mental environment. Finally, a weekly reflection ritual: What energized me? What drained me? What will I do differently next week? Self-awareness isn't accidental—it's scheduled.

"If you want a better life, build better loops."

Case Study: The Habit Audit That Saved a Pivot

Carla, a mid-career manager, was trying to pivot into entrepreneurship. She had the skills, the ideas, and the savings. But she couldn't find momentum. When we analyzed her routine, we discovered why: late-night Netflix until one in the morning, coffee-only mornings, constant multitasking, zero time for exercise or reflection.

We didn't overhaul her life—we performed habit surgery. Cut: late-night screens. Add: a ten-minute morning walk and five minutes of journaling. Replace: evening wine with tea and reading. Within six weeks, her energy doubled. Within three months, her business plan was done. Within a year, she'd launched. Her secret wasn't willpower. It was alignment.

Reflection Exercise: Your Habit Surgery Plan

In your journal, create two columns: To Cut (Saboteurs) and To Add (Keystones). Then answer: Which change would make the biggest difference in my energy or focus? What's the smallest step I can take to start today? How will I track it for the next thirty days?

Pick one cut and one add. Do them daily for thirty days. Anchor new habits to existing ones: After I brush my teeth, I journal for five minutes. After I make coffee, I stretch for three minutes. You're not inventing new routines—you're upgrading existing ones.

Closing Thought

Your pivot isn't powered by motivation. It's powered by momentum—and momentum is built by habits. Every day, you're performing one of two surgeries: installing vitality or removing it.

So make the cut. Install the new. Guard the habits that guard your growth. Because while life's big changes get the headlines, it's your small daily choices that write the story.

CHAPTER FIFTEEN

Funding the Transition

Turning Financial Fear into Freedom

> *"A career pivot without a money plan isn't courage—it's chaos. But with a plan, freedom becomes affordable."*

The Fear That Freezes Every Pivot

If you've ever felt trapped in a chapter that no longer fits, you've probably whispered some version of this: I'd love to make a change, but I can't afford to.

Those eight words are the most common reason people stay stuck—not fear of failure, not lack of clarity, not even self-doubt. Money anxiety is the number one pivot blocker. It's also the most solvable. When you master your financial strategy, you buy options. Options are freedom. Freedom is power. And power is what fuels your pivot.

The Real Cost of Staying Stuck

Before we talk about saving or budgeting, let's talk about loss. Every year you stay in a misaligned career carries a hidden price tag: lost income growth as your salary stagnates, lost compounding as your skills and potential stall, lost vitality as chronic stress erodes your health, and lost time—the one resource that never replenishes.

Staying stuck feels safe, but it's silently expensive. Freedom has a price, but stagnation has a mortgage. So instead of asking Can I afford to pivot? ask: Can I afford not to?

The Buffer Rule

Money buys runway, and runway buys peace of mind. When you have financial runway, you stop making fear-based decisions. You stop clinging to jobs you hate because you "need the stability." Runway creates emotional leverage—the time, space, and confidence to make your next move with intention rather than desperation.

Aim to save three to twelve months of living expenses, depending on the scale of your pivot. A small pivot in the same industry might need three months. A medium pivot—retraining or freelancing—warrants six to nine. A major life pivot—building a business, relocating, or taking a sabbatical—calls for six to twelve.

Let's make it tangible. If your monthly essentials total four thousand dollars, then three months of runway is twelve thousand, six months is twenty-four thousand, and twelve months is forty-eight thousand. That's your target. Build it systematically—dollar by dollar, week by week. Even a thousand dollars in a dedicated pivot fund changes your mindset from trapped to taking control.

*"Savings aren't just money in a bank—
they're courage in your pocket."*

Design Your Transition Timeline

A pivot without a timeline is just a wish. Map out the phases of your financial transition.

Phase One—Stability: secure your essentials, pay down high-interest debt, build baseline savings. Phase Two—Accumulation: increase income through side projects and redirect all surplus into your pivot fund. Phase Three—Transition: begin your pivot while maintaining financial discipline. Phase Four—Sustain: once your pivot generates reliable income, stabilize and rebuild long-term savings. Think of it like crossing a bridge: one foot in stability, one foot in motion, until you're safely on the other side.

The Mini-Sabbatical Strategy

High performers often test their pivots through mini-sabbaticals—intentional time blocks to experiment with their next path without burning their current bridge.

A sabbatical doesn't require moving to Bali. It might mean negotiating a four-week unpaid leave to explore a passion project, using vacation time for a trial run in a new role, or taking Fridays off for three months to work on a business idea. Most people underestimate how flexible employers can be when presented with a mature, professional plan. A well-designed mini-sabbatical reduces risk, reveals reality by testing your assumptions, and rebuilds the belief that change is possible.

"A mini-sabbatical is a rehearsal for your next life—without the curtain call."

Creative Funding Approaches

Not every pivot needs a pile of cash. Sometimes it just needs ingenuity.

First, a freelance or side hustle bridge: start generating income in your new direction before leaving your old one. Offer consulting, sell digital products, or take on small clients. Your goal isn't to replace your income immediately—it's to build proof and momentum.

Second, grants and fellowships. There are thousands of underused funding sources for adults changing careers or starting ventures. Search databases like GrantWatch for small business funding, Scholarships.com for adult learners, Hello Alice for female and minority entrepreneurs, and local business incubators offering seed grants.

Third, strategic downsizing. One of the fastest ways to buy time is to lower expenses—trading temporary comfort for long-term autonomy. Move to a cheaper rental for a year. Sell unused items. Eliminate forgotten subscriptions. Each dollar you stop spending is another day of freedom bought back. And before assuming you have to quit, check whether your employer offers tuition reimbursement, internal mobility programs, or consulting opportunities post-departure. Many companies would rather support your pivot than lose you completely.

"You don't always need more money—you just need more imagination."

Reframe Your Relationship with Money

This is where most people get stuck—not in math, but in mindset. Money isn't just numbers. It's emotion, identity, and story. You inherited beliefs about money from your parents, culture, and past—many of which quietly dictate your decisions.

If you've ever thought I'm just not good with money, or I need security above all else—those aren't truths. They're scripts. And they can be rewritten. Ask yourself: What beliefs about money did I grow up with? Which still serve me—and which are keeping me small? Your goal is to shift from fear-based thinking—I can't risk losing—to freedom-based thinking: I can afford to invest in myself.

"A pivot isn't reckless if you plan for it—it's an investment in your future self."

Build the Pivot Budget

A pivot budget isn't about restriction—it's about intention. Think of it in four buckets.

Essentials—housing, food, utilities, insurance—should take roughly fifty to sixty percent of income. Your pivot fund—savings for transition runway—should receive ten to twenty percent. Growth spending—learning, tools, professional development—deserves five to ten percent. And joy—experiences, rest, mental health—should get ten to fifteen percent. If you cut joy completely, your discipline won't last. Every dollar gets a destination. Automate transfers to your pivot fund on payday, even if it's just twenty-five dollars. Automation removes emotion—you pre-decide rather than negotiate with your goals each month.

Case Study: The Courage Fund

Maya was a marketing executive who wanted to pivot into nonprofit work. She made good money but was terrified of the pay cut. So instead of quitting impulsively, she created a Courage Fund.

Each month, she automated five hundred dollars into a separate account, cut subscriptions, paused luxury expenses, and freelanced one night a week. Within eighteen months, she had nine thousand dollars saved. That fund gave her enough runway to accept a nonprofit role that paid forty percent less. She's never been happier—and after a decade with the organization, they paid off her student loans. Her Courage Fund didn't just buy her freedom. It bought her peace.

A Personal Story: The Six-Month Runway That Changed Everything

When I decided to leave my corporate role to start CUnet, it wasn't a whimsical leap—it was a calculated pivot. I believed deeply in the idea: large colleges and universities were being taken advantage of by opaque agencies, and technology could fix it. But belief alone doesn't pay the bills.

Before I made the jump, I built a six-month runway—cash to cover all living expenses if the business made zero revenue in its first six months. No vacations, no luxury, just survival mode. I also had a backup plan: liquidate a few assets for another two months of buffer. And in the absolute worst case, I could move in temporarily with family. That thought alone lit a fire under me.

That runway didn't just fund my pivot—it fueled my confidence. It allowed me to think clearly, act boldly, and take risks strategically rather than desperately. The company started turning a profit in month six. Within two and a half years, CUnet went from concept to acquisition in the mid-eight figures. That's not luck. That's leverage. When you build financial runway, you're not just buying time—you're buying clarity, courage, and control.

Reflection Exercise: Your Pivot Funding Plan

Work through these five questions. How many months of expenses do you want saved? What's your target number? Where in your current spending can you cut or redirect toward your pivot fund? What small gigs or projects could supplement your savings? How will you automate transfers? And before each purchase this week, ask: Is this buying comfort or freedom?

Then write your declaration: I am funding my freedom, not my fear. Tape it somewhere visible. Because financial confidence isn't built overnight—it's built with every deliberate choice that says, I'm preparing for something bigger.

Closing Thought

You don't have to be rich to pivot. You just have to be ready. Pivots aren't irresponsible when planned—they're strategic when funded. Money, when aligned with purpose, is one of the most powerful creative forces on earth.

So don't fear it. Direct it. Build your buffer. Create your plan. Buy your freedom one deposit at a time. Because every dollar you save toward your next chapter is a down payment on your becoming.

"A pivot plan without a money plan is fantasy. With financial clarity, pivots become possible."

CHAPTER SIXTEEN

Communication Scripts

Speak Your Pivot into Existence

"How you explain your pivot shapes how others respond to it."

Why Words Matter

Your pivot doesn't just happen in your calendar or your finances—it happens in your conversations. You can plan, save, and prepare for months. But at some point, you'll have to tell someone. Your boss. Your partner. Your parents. Your team.

And in that moment, the way you communicate your decision will determine the tone of everything that follows. People don't just respond to what you say—they respond to how certain you sound when you say it. The stronger your language, the stronger their faith in your direction.

That's what this chapter is about: helping you speak your pivot into existence with clarity, confidence, and composure—even when your stomach's in knots.

"If you don't define your pivot, others will define it for you."

The Psychology of Announcing Change

When you make a big change, everyone around you goes through their own emotional reaction—curiosity, fear, projection, or even quiet envy. Your announcement stirs up their own relationship with risk and regret. Some people will be inspired. Others will be unsettled. A few will be judgmental.

That's not about you—it's about them. Your job isn't to manage their emotions. It's to manage your message. And the secret to doing that well is preparation. Scripts give you the language to handle tough conversations without spiraling into doubt or defensiveness.

The Golden Rule of Pivot Communication

Clarity + Confidence + Calm = Credibility. When you communicate your pivot, you're not asking for permission—you're sharing a decision. You're not seeking validation—you're offering transparency. The goal isn't to convince everyone that your pivot makes sense. It's to show that you've thought it through, planned for it, and are ready. That's the energy that earns respect, even from skeptics.

Script 1: Talking to Your Boss or Clients

When you're leaving a job, partnership, or professional commitment, the conversation is tricky because it mixes gratitude, closure, and boundaries. Your goal is to leave the bridge intact while walking confidently toward your next one.

Core message: "I've valued my time here, and I'm ready for a new chapter that aligns with my long-term vision."

In practice: "I want to start by saying how much I've appreciated the opportunities I've had here. This role has been a huge part of my growth, and I'm proud of what we've accomplished together. Over the last year, I've done some reflection and realized that my long-term vision is evolving. I'm ready to take on a new challenge that aligns more closely with that next phase. I wanted to be transparent and give as much notice as possible to ensure a smooth transition."

Lead with gratitude, not guilt. Speak in forward vision, not backward frustration. Avoid defensiveness—your pivot isn't a rejection; it's a realignment. End with an offer to help in the transition: "I'm happy to document processes, train a replacement, or stay connected if you ever want to collaborate down the road." Even if you never work together again, you'll be remembered as someone who left with grace.

"Leave the door open on your way out—
you never know when your future self
might need to walk back through it."

Script 2: Talking to Partners or Family

This is often the hardest conversation of all, because it's emotionally loaded. These are the people who worry about your safety, your income, and your future. They don't need convincing—they need confidence. When they feel your grounded conviction, their fear quiets.

Core message: "Here's why this matters to me, here's how I've planned for it, and here's how it benefits us."

In practice: "I want to share something important with you because it's been on my heart for a while. I've realized that what I'm doing now isn't where I want to be long-term. I've been planning this carefully—saving, preparing, and creating a realistic path forward. This isn't about running away from something; it's about building toward something better. I truly believe it will make me happier, healthier, and more present—which benefits both of us."

For a concerned partner, add: "I completely understand if this feels like a big shift. I've thought through the finances, the timeline, and the safety nets. I'm not taking this lightly—I'm taking it intentionally. I'd love for us to walk through it together." Partnership means inclusion, not surprise.

"You can't demand belief—you build it through transparency."

Script 3: Talking to Friends and Peers

This is where subtle judgment or envy can creep in. When you start making bold moves, it highlights other people's inertia. The trick is to disarm that defensiveness with authenticity.

Core message: "I'm trying something new—I'd love your support, and I'm open to feedback once I've tested it."

In practice: "I've decided to make a shift and try something new. I'm still figuring out the details, but I'm really excited about exploring this next chapter. I'd love your encouragement along the way. Once I've learned more, I'll share what's working—right now I'm just focused on getting started." Keep it light but confident. Don't overshare in the early stages; protect your energy while it's fragile.

"You don't owe everyone the details of your pivot—you owe yourself the space to grow into it."

Script 4: Responding to Critics and Skeptics

No matter how carefully you plan, not everyone will get it. Some will question your decision. Others will criticize out of fear or insecurity. Your instinct will be to defend yourself—but that's a trap. You don't owe anyone a debate.

Core message: "I appreciate your concern. I've thought it through." That's it. The more you explain, the more you feed their doubt—and yours.

In practice: "I understand why you might feel that way—it's definitely a big change. I've done my homework and feel good about the direction. Time will tell, but I'm excited about what's next." Calm. Neutral. Done. As Mark Twain observed: "Let us be thankful for the fools—but for them, the rest of us would not succeed." Let your results do the talking.

"The loudest answer to doubt is demonstrated success."

Script 5: Talking to Your Inner Critic

Let's be honest—sometimes the harshest critic isn't your boss, your partner, or your friend. It's you. The voice that whispers: Who do you think you are? What if this fails? You're too old, too young, too late.

That voice doesn't need to be silenced—it needs to be rewritten. Core message: "Thank you for trying to keep me safe. But I'm safe now, and growing requires risk." In practice: "I know you're scared, and that's okay. You're trying to protect me from failure and embarrassment. But I've done the planning, I've prepared the path, and I'm choosing growth over comfort. We've stayed still long enough—it's time to move forward."

This inner dialogue might feel strange at first, but it's essential. If you don't learn to talk to your fear, you'll keep talking from it.

> *"Your pivot won't fall apart from external criticism—it'll stall from internal hesitation."*

Three Tone Archetypes

There isn't just one right way to communicate a pivot. Three archetypes are worth keeping in mind.

The Visionary uses a bold, confident, future-oriented tone—best when announcing publicly or inspiring others. The Diplomat speaks with calm, respectful, inclusive language—best with bosses, partners, or family. The Rebel is direct, unapologetic, and fiery—best when reclaiming identity or breaking free from toxic patterns.

You can blend them: a Diplomat at work, a Visionary online, a Rebel with yourself. Authenticity is the only non-negotiable.

The Pivot Announcement Checklist

Before communicating your change, confirm five things. Clarity: Am I clear on my why and my plan? Confidence: Do I believe in what I'm saying? Timing: Is now the right moment to share? Boundaries: How much am I choosing to reveal? Tone: Does this reflect my calm conviction, not my anxiety? Once those are locked in—speak your truth.

Case Study: The Power of Framing

Alex had spent twelve years in corporate sales but wanted to launch a coaching business. He dreaded telling his boss, imagining disappointment or the label of ingratitude.

Instead of making it emotional, he framed it strategically: "I've loved being part of this team and learning from everyone here. I've realized I want to take what I've learned and apply it in a new way—helping others develop the same skills that helped me succeed here. My plan is to build this gradually and transition responsibly."

The result? His boss congratulated him—and referred his first client. It wasn't what Alex said. It was how he said it: with clarity, respect, and conviction.

Reflection Exercise: Write Your Pivot Script

Grab your journal and complete this framework: "Over the past [timeframe], I've realized that [area of life] no longer aligns with my long-term goals. I've thought through this carefully, saved and planned, and I'm ready to take the next step toward [new direction]. I'm grateful for what this chapter taught me and excited for what's next."

Practice saying it aloud—to the mirror, to a friend, or record yourself. You'll notice something powerful: each time you say it, your conviction grows. By the fifth repetition, your tone shifts from hopeful to certain. And certainty is contagious.

Closing Thought

Announcing your pivot isn't just communication—it's commitment. Each conversation is a line in the sand between who you were and who you're becoming.

You don't need everyone's blessing to move forward. You just need your own conviction—spoken clearly, calmly, and consistently. Because in the end, words aren't just how you share your pivot. They're how you cement it.

"Scripts don't eliminate nerves—they eliminate confusion. Speak with clarity, and your confidence will follow."

Chapter Seventeen

Managing the Dip

The Valley Between Excitement and Breakthrough

"Every pivot has a Dip—the space between what was and what will be. It's not failure. It's the forge."

The Emotional Rollercoaster of Change

If the beginning of a pivot is a spark, the middle is often smoke.

At first, you're on fire with inspiration. You've noticed the signals, made the decision, built a plan, and started moving. You feel alive again—free, brave, unstoppable. Then suddenly, one morning, it hits you: you're exhausted. The excitement feels distant. The results aren't here yet. The fear is louder than before.

Welcome to the Dip. It's not a glitch in your journey—it is your journey. The Dip is where enthusiasm fades, uncertainty peaks, and transformation actually begins. Most pivots die here. But it's also where the few who persevere are reborn.

The Three Stages of Every Pivot

Whether you're changing careers, leaving a relationship, healing your body, or rebuilding your identity—every major transformation follows a predictable arc.

Stage One is the Honeymoon Phase: when everything feels new and exciting. Stage Two is the Dip: when progress slows and reality sets in. Stage Three is the Recovery: when momentum rebuilds and results finally appear. Understanding these phases helps you normalize the chaos instead of misinterpreting it as failure.

Stage 1: The Honeymoon Phase

At the start of any big change, energy surges. You're high on clarity, passion, and possibility. You wake up early, bursting with motivation. You tell friends and family. You picture your success vividly.

This phase is powerful and necessary. It's what gives you the courage to leap. But it's also temporary. The human brain is wired to crave novelty. When something feels fresh, dopamine spikes. As novelty wears off and effort increases, dopamine dips—and reality steps in.

"The start of every pivot feels like flying—until gravity reminds you that growth takes work."

Stage 2: The Dip

This is the emotional valley between old comfort and new confidence. One day you realize: the results aren't matching your effort. The people who cheered you at the start have gone quiet. The routines you built now feel like chores. Doubt sneaks in, whispering, Maybe I made a mistake.

The Dip happens because dopamine drops as novelty fades, because you're no longer comparing to the past but confronting the future, and because change takes longer, costs more, and demands more energy than expected. Your old identity is dissolving, but the new one isn't stable yet. That's what makes the Dip feel like drowning—you're between shores, treading water, wondering whether to swim back.

You might hear yourself saying: I thought I'd be further along by now. This was easier in my head. I miss my old life, even though I hated it. Why do I feel so tired all the time? Maybe this just isn't for me.

If any of those sound familiar—you're not broken. You're growing. The Dip isn't a detour. It's the developmental phase between the old version of you and the one you're becoming.

"The Dip is not a wall. It's a tunnel. Keep moving—there's light ahead."

Stage 3: The Recovery

If you stay the course, something beautiful happens. Small wins appear. Momentum rebuilds. You realize you're stronger than you thought and smarter than you feared.

This stage isn't euphoric like the Honeymoon Phase. It's deeper, steadier. It's the quiet confidence that comes from earning your progress, not imagining it.

You've gone from believing in your pivot to embodying it.

Four Tools to Survive the Dip

1. Anchor to Your Pivot Thesis

When you crafted your Pivot Thesis (Chapter 9), you wrote your why now, your what changes, and your success criteria. That thesis is your anchor. During the Dip, you'll question everything. Pull it out. Read it daily —especially on the days you feel like quitting.

"When the path feels foggy, reread your map."

---

2. Celebrate Micro-Wins

In the Dip, big progress feels invisible—so you must magnify the small stuff. Did you make a single healthy choice today? Send that email you've been avoiding? Show up even though you didn't want to? That's victory. Track your wins. Journal them. Reward yourself with acknowledgment. Remember: evidence defeats disbelief.

3. Lean on Your Pivot Crew

This is when your Pivot Crew becomes invaluable. When motivation dips, connection sustains. Call your mentor. Text your accountability partner. Share your fears honestly. Don't isolate. Isolation magnifies doubt; connection dissolves it. The right people won't just cheer for you—they'll remind you who you are when you forget.

"Borrow belief from your crew until your own returns."

4. Remember the Cost of Staying Still

When you're tempted to quit, revisit Chapter 1. Remind yourself of the pain you left behind—the misalignment, the exhaustion, the quiet dread. You didn't pivot because it was easy. You pivoted because staying still was unbearable.

As President Kennedy observed, there are risks and costs to a program of action—but they are far less than the long-range risks and costs of comfortable inaction. Don't let short-term discomfort trick you into long-term regret.

"The Dip hurts—but not as much as staying stuck."

Case Study: The Dip in Real Life

The Career Pivot

James left a high-paying finance job to become a startup founder. The first two months were exhilarating. The third month was terrifying. Clients didn't come fast enough. Bills piled up. His self-esteem plummeted.

He almost gave up—until he re-read his Pivot Thesis: I want to create something that helps others succeed financially, not just profit for profit's sake. He pushed through, focused on small wins, and leaned on his mentor weekly. A year later, he wasn't just profitable—

he was peaceful. "The Dip didn't mean I was failing. It meant I was learning what my old job never taught me —resilience."

The Relationship Pivot

Lena ended a long-term relationship that was safe but stagnant. At first, she felt powerful. Then came loneliness, self-doubt, and endless "what ifs." She almost went back—not because she wanted him, but because she missed the familiar.

Then she re-read her notes from Chapter 1: the list of what she was losing by staying still. She realized that comfort isn't love—it's sedation. Six months later, she wasn't back with him. She was back with herself.

The Health Pivot

Anthony decided to stop drinking and get healthy. The first two weeks were euphoric—the honeymoon of change. Then came cravings, mood swings, social pressure, and fatigue. He hit the Dip hard. Instead of giving up, he joined a support group, tracked his streaks, and celebrated every sober Friday like a championship. Today, he's eighteen months alcohol-free and in the best shape since he was a high school athlete. "The Dip felt endless, but it was only temporary. My new life isn't perfect, but it's mine."

How to Shorten the Dip

You can't skip it, but you can shorten it.

Expect it. Anticipation disarms anxiety—knowing the Dip is coming makes it less frightening. Name it. Labeling the phase creates distance: This is just the Dip. It's happening, but it's not me, and it's not permanent. Simplify. In the Dip, complexity kills momentum—focus on one daily non-negotiable. Refuel. Prioritize sleep, nutrition, and self-care. The Dip drains energy, and your body needs fuel. Seek proof. Review your wins, journal progress, or talk to someone already on the other side. And recommit daily: This is the price of progress, and I can afford it.

"The Dip doesn't test your talent. It tests your tolerance for uncertainty."

The Pivot Equation: Grit × Grace

To move through the Dip, you need two forces in balance. Grit is the discipline to keep going when it's not fun. Grace is the compassion to rest when it's too heavy.

Too much grit and you burn out. Too much grace and you drift. The sweet spot is the blend—persistent yet patient. That's how you outlast the Dip without losing yourself in it.

Reflection Exercise: The Dip Journal

Grab your notebook and complete this reflection: What Dip am I currently in? What emotions am I feeling right now? What proof do I have that I'm making progress, even if it's small? What's one thing I can celebrate today? Who can I reach out to for perspective or encouragement?

Revisit this exercise weekly. Tracking your Dip turns it from chaos into curriculum.

Closing Thought

Every meaningful transformation has its valley—the Dip between excitement and reward. But the Dip isn't a verdict. It's a rite of passage.

Anchor to your purpose. Celebrate your smallest wins. Lean on your people. And never forget why you started. Because once you walk through the Dip—with grit, grace, and faith—you'll realize something profound: you were never lost. You were just leveling up.

"The Dip is not a sign you're failing—it's proof you're growing. Push through, and the rewards multiply."

Part Four

Sustain

Living the Pivoted Life

Making a pivot isn't the end of the story—it's the beginning of a new way of living. The real challenge is sustaining momentum, ensuring the pivot continues to serve you, and allowing it to ripple outward into the lives of others.

Part IV focuses on long-term fulfillment. It's about measuring progress not only in external results, but in purpose, energy, and joy. It's about building real-time feedback loops so you don't drift back into autopilot. It's about recognizing that pivots are not one-time events, but part of a lifelong rhythm of growth. And finally, it's about living in such alignment that your pivots leave a lasting legacy on the people and communities around you.

Chapters in Part Four

Chapter Eighteen

Measuring Fulfillment

Redefining Success from the Inside Out

"You can't feel fulfilled using someone else's scorecard."

The Lie of the Old Scorecard

We live in a world obsessed with measurement. We measure income, followers, titles, steps, calories, and likes. But we've built precision around the wrong things.

The old scorecard of success—money, status, possessions—measures accumulation, not alignment. It tells you how much you have, but not how alive you feel. For years, maybe decades, most of us have been chasing that outdated scorecard, assuming that one day, when the numbers are high enough, fulfillment will finally arrive. It doesn't. Because fulfillment isn't earned through numbers—it's experienced through alignment.

"Achievement feeds the ego. Alignment feeds the soul."

The Problem with Old Metrics

You've probably felt it: the promotion that didn't fix the emptiness. The purchase that lost its thrill in a week. The compliment that faded faster than the doubt beneath it.

That's because the old metrics—salary, title, accolades—are lagging indicators of success. They reflect what you've done, not how you feel doing it. Fulfillment requires leading indicators: signals that you're on the right path as you walk it. This chapter gives you a new system: the Fulfillment Scorecard, a simple, science-backed way to measure alignment and joy, not just achievement.

The Three Fulfillment Metrics

Fulfillment is multidimensional, but it can be distilled into three powerful metrics: Purpose (meaning and contribution), Energy (vitality and engagement), and Joy (gratitude and emotional richness). Together, they form your internal GPS.

1. Purpose: The Meaning Metric

Question: Am I working on something meaningful to me? Purpose is the sense that your effort matters—that your time, energy, and pain are building toward something significant. It doesn't have to be grand. It just has to matter to you.

Maybe your purpose is raising a child, building a business, teaching others, writing, creating, healing, or simply living with integrity. Whatever it is, purpose gives pain a reason. It turns obstacles into challenges and effort into fulfillment.

Measure it weekly or monthly by asking: Do I feel proud of what I'm contributing? Do my daily actions reflect what I value? Would I still care about this if nobody noticed? Rate it 1 to 10. A 10 doesn't mean perfection—it means alignment. When purpose is low, fatigue skyrockets, because you're burning energy without meaning.

To raise your purpose score: reconnect with why you started. Say no to activities that don't fit your core values. Ask, Who benefits from my work? Reframe dull tasks as contributions to a larger mission. Purpose is the antidote to burnout.

"When you lose purpose, even rest won't refresh you."

---

2. Energy: The Vitality Metric

Question: Do my days fuel me or drain me? Energy is your body's emotional feedback system. If you constantly feel exhausted—not from effort or exercise, but from existence—it's a sign that something's misaligned. The goal isn't endless stamina; it's energy integrity: where what you give and what you get are in balance.

Measure it by asking: Do I wake up excited or dreading the day? What activities drain me most, and which recharge me? How do I feel after spending time with certain people or tasks? Rate it 1 to 10. A low score doesn't mean you're lazy—it means your energy is being misallocated.

To raise your energy score: audit daily tasks and eliminate, automate, or delegate drains. Move your body every day—motion creates emotion. Guard your sleep and nutrition. Build white space into your calendar for rest and reflection. Replace energy vampires with energy chargers.

"Alignment doesn't just look good on paper—it feels good in your body."

---

3. Joy: The Gratitude Metric

Question: How often do I feel real gratitude, flow, or excitement? Joy isn't the same as pleasure or comfort. Pleasure is fleeting; joy is sustainable. Joy shows up when you're fully present, authentic, and grateful—when you stop performing and start being.

You know that feeling when you lose track of time, when you're laughing, creating, or connecting deeply? That's joy—the ultimate sign of alignment. Measure it by asking: How often do I smile, laugh, or feel at peace? When was the last time I felt truly grateful? How much of my week felt like flow versus force?

To raise your joy score: practice daily gratitude—three moments, no matter how small. Schedule play or creativity (yes, schedule it). Reduce comparison, which kills joy faster than almost anything. Be where your feet are—presence is joy's oxygen. Joy isn't a luxury. It's a metric of health. You don't earn it later—you cultivate it now.

"Joy isn't what happens when life's perfect. It's what happens when you stop demanding that it be."

The Fulfillment Scorecard

Combine these three metrics into one system: your Fulfillment Scorecard. Once a month, rate yourself 1 to 10 on each of the three dimensions—Purpose, Energy, and Joy. Total your three numbers, divide by three, and that's your Fulfillment Index. Write it down. Notice trends.

The goal isn't a perfect 10. It's improvement and awareness. Over time, you'll notice something remarkable: when your alignment rises, your anxiety falls. If your scores read 5, 4, and 3 in January, then 6, 5, and 6 in February, and 8, 7, and 7 in March—the numbers tell a story. The real insight comes from the patterns: the dips and rises, and what drove them.

"You can't improve what you don't measure—even when it comes to meaning."

The Fulfillment Flywheel

When the three metrics reinforce each other, a self-sustaining loop forms. When Purpose rises, you become more motivated—and Energy increases. When Energy rises, you engage more deeply—and Joy increases. When Joy rises, gratitude expands—and Purpose feels clearer.

This is the fulfillment flywheel, originally described by Jim Collins as a concept of momentum building on itself. Your goal isn't to max all three overnight—it's to keep the wheel turning. Fulfillment, like fitness, improves through attention and iteration.

Integrating the Scorecard into Your Life

Set aside twenty minutes on the last Sunday of every month. Score yourself on each metric and write one paragraph about each score: What improved this month? What drained me? What can I tweak next month? Keep a simple log—journal, spreadsheet, or app. Over time, you'll see clear links between your habits and your happiness.

Each quarter, choose one area to focus on improving. For example: This quarter, I'll increase my Energy score by prioritizing rest.

Use the scorecard to manage alignment the way great leaders manage organizations—with data, reflection, and course correction. But instead of maximizing profit, you're maximizing happiness, peace, and contentment.

"Fulfillment isn't a finish line. It's a dashboard."

Reflection Exercise: Your Fulfillment Audit

Write down the following: What currently gives my life meaning? What activities, people, or projects drain my energy? What moments recently sparked real joy or gratitude? How would my daily life look if my Purpose, Energy, and Joy were all 9s? What's one small shift I can make this week to raise one score by one point?

Repeat monthly. You'll be amazed at how awareness alone changes your actions.

Closing Thought

You've measured your finances. Tracked your performance. Monitored your progress. Now it's time to measure what actually matters.

Because success without fulfillment is failure in disguise. And fulfillment, once tracked and nurtured, becomes your truest compass—guiding you not just to achievement, but to aliveness. Create your scorecard. Check it monthly. Adjust when needed. Because your goal isn't to live the longest life possible—it's to live the most aligned one.

"Fulfillment becomes measurable—making it easier to stay aligned long-term."

Chapter Nineteen

Course-Correcting in Real Time

The Art of Staying Aligned While You Move

"You don't set your life once. You steer it."

The Myth of the Perfect Pivot

Many people treat a pivot like a destination—as if once you make it, you've arrived. But that's not how real change works. A pivot isn't a one-time event. It's an ongoing relationship with direction.

Even after you've left the job, started the business, ended the relationship, or changed your habits, you'll still encounter drift—tiny shifts that pull you off course without you realizing it. It's not failure. It's physics. Every system, including you, requires course correction to stay true.

"A rocket on its way to the moon is off-course most of the time—but constant micro-adjustments get it there."

Life as a Flight Path

Imagine you're the pilot of a plane. You take off confidently, destination in sight. But mid-flight, winds change, turbulence hits, visibility drops. If you don't adjust, you'll drift miles off target.

The same is true for life. Your vision is the destination. Your habits are the controls. Your feedback loops are the navigation system. If you're not checking your coordinates, you're flying blind—even if you started strong.

Why Course-Correction Matters

Pivots bring freedom, but freedom without reflection turns into chaos. You start a new business but work creeps back into eighty-hour weeks. You leave a toxic relationship but repeat the same patterns. You prioritize health but slip into burnout chasing "optimization."

Without regular recalibration, your new life slowly morphs into your old one—just with different packaging. Real-time course correction keeps your life intentional instead of reactive.

"Without reflection, even freedom becomes another form of autopilot."

Step 1: Build Feedback Loops

Feedback loops are simple: input, reflection, adjustment. In life, this means regularly asking yourself: What's working? What feels off? What feedback am I ignoring? What is life trying to teach me right now?

Build them into your week. Every Sunday, ask: When did I feel most alive this week? When did I feel drained?

That's your emotional GPS recalibrating. Monthly, review your Fulfillment Scorecard from Chapter 18—if one metric is trending down, that's a signal, not a shame.

Every ninety days, zoom out for a deep dive: What's working beautifully? What's no longer serving me? What small course correction would bring me back into alignment? By creating consistent reflection rhythms, you'll never drift too far from true north.

Step 2: Quarterly Self-Reviews

Treat your life like your most valuable project—because it is. Set aside one afternoon every three months. Go offline. Make it sacred.

Ask yourself six questions. What worked this quarter? What actions, habits, or relationships fueled progress? What felt off or forced? Where did I resist growth? What have I learned? What will I release? And what will I double down on, because it produces disproportionate fulfillment? You don't need to overhaul everything. One honest review can prevent years of quiet drift.

"Reflection isn't self-indulgence—it's navigation."

Step 3: Micro-Pivots

A micro-pivot is a small, strategic adjustment that realigns you without uprooting everything. Think of them as course corrections, not reinventions.

Adjusting your sleep routine. Delegating a draining task. Setting a new boundary with a client or friend. Renegotiating a commitment. Reallocating time toward something energizing. Small shifts compound fast. You don't need to burn your life down to rebuild it. You just need to keep tweaking it toward alignment.

In aviation, a plane that's just one degree off course ends up sixty miles off target after flying three thousand miles. Life works the same way. Tiny misalignments, tolerated long enough, lead to massive regret. Tiny corrections, applied consistently, lead to massive fulfillment.

"You don't fix a life by blowing it up. You fix it by fine-tuning it."

Step 4: Watch for Drift

Life's default setting is drift. It's what happens when you stop paying attention. You don't notice it at first. Then one day you realize you've built a life optimized for someone else's priorities again.

Signs you're drifting: You're busy but not satisfied. You're achieving goals that no longer excite you. You feel guilty saying no but resentful saying yes. You're nostalgic for the version of yourself that took risks. Drift isn't laziness—it's a lack of awareness. The antidote is regular reflection and recalibration.

"If you don't design your days, your days will design you."

Step 5: Your Life Alignment Dashboard

We live in an age of dashboards—fitness apps, bank balances, productivity trackers. Build one for your life.

Six categories worth tracking monthly or quarterly, each with a simple check-in question and a trend arrow: **Purpose—Am I still working on what matters to me? Energy—Do I feel energized by my days? Joy—Am I present and grateful? Relationships—Are my connections nourishing or draining? Health—Am I moving, eating, and resting well? Finances—Am I buying freedom or stress?** Visual data transforms vague intuition into clear insight. This is how you manage alignment like an asset.

Step 6: Re-evaluate Your Goals

Course correction isn't just about fixing problems—it's about evolving with purpose. Sometimes what once felt right no longer fits. That's not failure; it's growth.

Every few months, ask: Are my goals still mine, or just old momentum? Does this still feel like expansion, or obligation? If I were starting from scratch today, would I choose this? If not, pivot. Even slightly. Because you're not who you were when you started—and that's the point.

"The goal of a pivot isn't to stay the same somewhere new—it's to evolve into someone truer."

Celebrate Course Corrections

Most people only celebrate big achievements. But the real growth lies in the small, quiet decisions—the moment you notice drift and choose to realign. Every time you do, you strengthen the muscle of awareness.

The moment you say no to what's wrong. The moment you rest instead of push. The moment you update your plan instead of abandoning it. That's mastery—not perfection, but presence. Celebrate those moments. They're proof that you're awake at the wheel of your life.

Reflection Exercise: The 90-Day Alignment Review

At the end of each quarter, answer: What am I most proud of this quarter? What drained me the most? What am I tolerating that I shouldn't be? What am I craving that I've been avoiding? What's one degree I can shift to feel more aligned next quarter?

Write it down. Commit to one change. That's how you compound alignment over time.

Closing Thought

Every pivot is a starting line, not a finish. The world changes. You change. Your needs change. That's not instability—that's evolution.

Your job isn't to find one perfect path and freeze there. It's to stay awake, adaptable, and aligned as you go. Check your gauges. Review your map. Adjust your altitude. The secret to a life well lived isn't rigidity. It's responsiveness.

"Real-time adjustments prevent small misalignments from becoming major regrets."

CHAPTER TWENTY

When One Pivot Leads to Another

Evolving Without Losing Yourself

> *"One pivot often opens the door to another. The goal isn't to keep spinning—it's to keep aligning."*

The Chain Reaction of Change

When you make one significant change in life, it rarely stays contained. You quit a draining job, and suddenly you care about your health again. You start taking care of your body, and your relationships improve. You end an unhealthy relationship, and you rediscover a creativity you thought was lost.

Every pivot creates a ripple. At first it feels accidental—like you fixed one thing and stumbled into ten more. But over time, you realize: each new layer of alignment reveals the next. Your career pivot exposes your health misalignment. Your health pivot exposes your relational imbalances. Your relational pivot exposes your mindset blocks. The process is endless because evolution is endless.

"Alignment isn't a destination. It's a rhythm."

Healthy Evolution vs. Pivot Addiction

There's a difference between growth and escape. Healthy evolution is when you pivot to expand your capacity for joy, freedom, or alignment. Pivot addiction is when you pivot to avoid discomfort, boredom, or self-confrontation. The first leads to peace. The second leads to exhaustion.

There's a rush that comes with new beginnings—the feeling of being alive again, curious, brave. But constant reinvention without integration turns life into a loop: always chasing, never landing. Because while change is exciting, stability is what gives change meaning.

"Reinvention is powerful. Integration is peace."

The Signs of Pivot Addiction

You're chasing pivots instead of embodying them when: you crave the rush of starting over more than the satisfaction of follow-through; you leave situations the moment they stop being easy or exciting; you justify constant change as growth but feel increasingly scattered or fatigued; you often burn bridges instead of building transitions; you fear stillness, because stillness forces reflection.

If you see yourself here, don't shame yourself—awareness is step one. You don't need fewer pivots. You need purposeful ones.

"A healthy pivot expands your roots—not uproots your peace."

The Power of Integration

Every pivot comes with lessons, but most people rush past them. They treat the pivot as a fix, not a teacher.

Each pivot is a classroom. Your career pivot teaches courage and clarity. Your health pivot teaches consistency and self-worth. Your relationship pivot teaches communication and boundaries. If you don't integrate those lessons, you'll repeat them—just in new forms.

Integration is how you honor your growth. Reflect on what this change taught you. Refine what you'll do differently. Root yourself in the habits and mindsets that will sustain this new chapter. Rest—give yourself time to stabilize before the next change. The more you integrate, the less reactive your life becomes and the more intentional your evolution.

"Every pivot is a teacher. Integration is how you graduate."

Practical Ways to Stay Balanced

Establish stability anchors: morning routines, mindfulness practices, or journaling that keep you grounded through transition. Relationships or mentors that reflect your growth honestly. Consistent self-checks to prevent unnecessary pivots.

After a major life change, commit to no new pivots for ninety days. Use that time to integrate, stabilize, and recalibrate. The wisdom behind this mirrors what recovery programs teach: when you're undergoing deep transformation, your system—emotionally, mentally, and physically—needs stability before adding new variables.

Redefine success to include peaceful consistency. Ask yourself: Can I enjoy the quiet without needing to stir the pot? And shift from chasing to cultivating—instead of searching for the next pivot, ask: How can I deepen this one? What can I master here before moving on?

"Stillness is not stagnation. It's digestion."

Case Study: Two Paths

The Cascade of Growth

After leaving her corporate job to start a creative business, Julia thought she was just changing careers. But the more aligned her work became, the more misaligned other areas felt. She realized she was in a relationship that didn't support her growth. She had been neglecting her health. She had friends who only knew the old version of her.

Her one pivot became five—but this wasn't chaos; it was coherence. Each change was a domino of alignment, building a life that finally matched her inner evolution.

The Restless Changer

Meanwhile, Ryan prided himself on always evolving. Every six to twelve months, he changed jobs, diets, and social circles, justifying it as growth. But underneath, he was chasing novelty to escape discomfort. He never stayed long enough to absorb the deeper lessons each change offered.

Eventually he hit burnout—not from effort, but from emotional fragmentation. His real growth began when he stopped chasing the next thing and started committing to mastery of one. He learned that peace is a form of progress too.

"Evolution isn't about doing more. It's about doing deeper."

The Lifecycle of a Pivot

Every pivot follows a natural rhythm: noticing misalignment, deciding to change, moving forward, navigating the Dip, stabilizing the shift, integrating the lessons—and then noticing again as new misalignments emerge.

That's the rhythm of an intentional life. You're not failing when you pivot again. You're living consciously—revising your map as you learn the terrain.

Reflection Exercise: The Pivot Chain Audit

Write down your recent pivots—large or small. For each, ask: What did this pivot teach me? What did it reveal that still needs attention? Have I integrated the lessons, or am I already chasing the next thing? Is my next change born of expansion or avoidance? Where in my life could I stay and deepen instead of move and start over?

Closing Thought

Pivots are not just about movement—they're about becoming. And sometimes, becoming requires stillness, reflection, and the humility to say, This is enough for now.

Yes, one pivot often leads to another—because growth exposes growth. But your job isn't to keep spinning in endless motion. Your job is to listen: to notice when life invites change and when it invites calm. To know when to shift and when to stay. When to build and when to breathe.

Because in the end, the goal isn't endless pivots. It's a life of perpetual alignment—evolving without losing your center.

"Normalize evolution—but balance it with rootedness. The goal isn't endless pivots. It's aligned living."

Chapter Twenty-One

Legacy on Your Terms

How Living Aligned Creates Ripples That Outlast You

"You may never know who needed you to pivot —but someone did."

Beyond You: The Invisible Ripples of Your Choices

Every pivot begins as a personal act—a decision between you and your own truth. But your decision doesn't stop with you.

Every time you choose courage over comfort, authenticity over approval, and purpose over fear—someone is watching. Your children. Your peers. Your friends. Your team. Your community. And in your quiet act of change, they see something revolutionary: permission. Permission to question. Permission to evolve. Permission to start again.

Because when you live pivoted, you become living proof that transformation is possible—not in theory, but in practice.

"Your legacy isn't what you leave when you're gone. It's what you give while

---

you're here through the example of a life fully lived."

Legacy Isn't Later—It's Now

Too often, people think of legacy as something far off—an obituary word, reserved for the end of a career or a lifetime. But your legacy isn't something you leave behind someday. It's something you're building today.

It's not just in what you achieve, but in how you choose. Every pivot—every brave realignment—becomes a building block in that legacy. You don't have to be famous to leave one. You just have to live consciously enough that your courage leaves an imprint.

The Ripple Effect of Courage

Think back to the people who inspired your own changes. Maybe it was a mentor who left a "safe" career to follow purpose. A friend who broke a toxic cycle and found peace. A leader who chose integrity over popularity. Chances are, their decision gave you courage.

Your pivot—even if quiet—is contagious. It shows others that they can survive reinvention, too. Courage breeds courage.

"When you choose alignment, you unconsciously grant others permission to do the same."

Case Studies in Ripple

The Corporate Mother

Melissa was a VP at a global company. Her dream was to start a wellness practice, but she worried what her kids would think if she "gave up" her stable job. She finally made the leap. Within a year, her daughter told her: "Mom, watching you do this made me realize I don't have to settle either." That's legacy—not a title, but a transfer of courage.

The Midlife Reinventor

John, fifty-two, pivoted from finance to teaching. His former colleagues thought he'd lost it—until one of them called months later and said: "You made me realize I've been miserable for years. I'm finally taking the leap too." Every time you act from authenticity, you give others the map out of their own stuckness.

Redefining Legacy: From Reputation to Resonance

Reputation is what people say about you. Legacy is what people carry from you. Your real legacy is how you made people feel seen, how you modeled self-trust, how you handled the hard things with grace, how you lived in alignment even when it was inconvenient.

Maya Angelou transformed personal pain into universal poetry, teaching dignity and courage. Fred Rogers made generations of children feel seen and emotionally safe, and his influence outlasted him in how those children treated each other. Legacy lives not in monuments but in moments—in the subtle shift a person carries from knowing you.

"Legacy is less about leaving something behind and more about leaving people changed."

The Fear of "Too Late"

Many people, especially in midlife, fear it's too late to pivot—that their legacy is already written. It's not. Legacy isn't built backward; it's built forward.

Some of the world's most inspiring reinventions happened after forty, fifty, even seventy. Colonel Sanders franchised KFC at sixty-two. Vera Wang designed her first dress at forty. Ray Kroc founded McDonald's at fifty-two. Laura Ingalls Wilder published her first Little House book at sixty-five. Arianna Huffington co-founded The Huffington Post at fifty-five. Barbara Taylor Bradford published her first novel at forty-six—and went on to sell over ninety million copies. Taikichiro Mori left academia at fifty-five to start a real estate firm and became the world's richest man within decades. Rodney Dangerfield returned to comedy in his mid-fifties after a decade selling aluminum siding.

Their success lay not just in the fame, but in the courage to pivot when everyone else thought the script was finished. Legacy starts the moment you decide your story isn't over.

"Legacy doesn't care when you start. It only cares that you start."

Passing It Forward

You don't need a platform to pass your legacy forward. You just need intention.

Model transparency—talk openly about your pivots not as wins, but as learning experiences. Mentor generously—help one person who's where you once were. Build something that outlasts you—a process, a story, a tool, a mindset. It doesn't have to be massive; it just has to matter. Normalize reinvention in your circles —speak about change as growth, not crisis. And celebrate others' pivots. Every time someone around you evolves, affirm it. Encouragement keeps the ripple alive.

Reflection Exercise: The Legacy Letter

Write a short letter titled Legacy on My Terms. Address it to your future self or to someone you love. In it, write what you've learned from your pivots, what you hope those choices teach others, and what kind of world you want your courage to help create. Sign it. Date it. Keep it where you'll see it once a year.

Closing Thought

You've learned how to Notice, Decide, Move, and Sustain. You've redefined success, reclaimed alignment, and rebuilt your life from the inside out. Now the question isn't just how you'll live—it's how your living will impact others.

Because a pivot is never just a turn in your path. It's a turning point in someone else's belief about what's possible. That's legacy. Not wealth. Not fame. Not perfection. But the ripple of a life that said: I refused to live on autopilot. I chose to live awake.

"The final payoff of pivoting is not just your own fulfillment—but the permission you grant others to live their truth."

CHAPTER TWENTY-TWO

The Big Pivots of Life

Different Paths, Same Permission

> *"Every major change in life begins the same way—with a whisper that says, 'This isn't it anymore.'"*

By now, you understand that a pivot is not about quitting—it's about realigning. It's not just about career shifts or life overhauls, but about listening to truth wherever it's calling you. The framework of Notice → Decide → Move → Sustain applies universally to any major life domain.

This chapter is a tour through the biggest pivot arenas most people face at some point in their lives. You don't need to tackle them all—but by recognizing these patterns, you'll see how the same principles echo everywhere.

1. Career & Work: Redefining Success

We spend nearly a third of our lives working. When the work that once energized you starts to drain you—when you've climbed a ladder leaning against the wrong wall—that's the call for a career pivot. Maybe it means changing industries, starting something of your own, or redefining your role. Your value doesn't vanish when you change direction. It compounds.

Notice: I dread Mondays. I feel invisible in meetings. Decide: It's not failure to want something different—it's honesty. Move: Start small—informational interviews, side projects, experiments. Sustain: Rebuild your identity around your adaptability and passion, not your title.

"You're not starting over. You're starting deeper."

2. Relationships: Redefining Connection

Sometimes you outgrow dynamics that once fit perfectly. A relationship pivot doesn't always mean ending something—often it means redefining it. From codependence to healthy interdependence. From silence to communication. From tolerance to authentic intimacy.

Notice: We're repeating patterns that don't feel good anymore. Decide: I want connection that nurtures growth, not fear. Move: Start the conversation. Suggest therapy. Establish new boundaries. Sustain: Practice honesty even when it's uncomfortable.

"Sometimes love requires letting go of the version of each other that no longer fits."

3. Health & Wellness: Returning to Wholeness

Your body is the vehicle of your purpose. A health pivot can mean adopting new habits, healing a toxic relationship with food or exercise, quitting substances, or simply prioritizing rest after years of burnout. Health pivots are rarely about weight or image—they're about self-respect.

Notice: I'm always tired. I'm short-tempered. My body is trying to tell me something. Decide: I want vitality, not just survival. Move: Start with one change—hydration, walking, or sleep. Sustain: Make your wellness practices part of who you are, not just what you do.

"Self-care isn't indulgence—it's maintenance for your mission."

---

4. Financial: Redefining Security

A financial pivot might mean downsizing, changing your relationship with consumption, rethinking investments, or creating income streams that align with your values. The goal isn't just more money—it's better money: money that supports your freedom, not your fear.

Notice: I'm earning more, but feeling less. Decide: My spending should reflect my values, not my insecurities. Move: Audit your habits. Simplify. Create a six- to twelve-month runway for flexibility. Sustain: Track not just dollars, but peace of mind. As Epictetus observed, wealth consists not in having great possessions, but in having few wants.

5. Beliefs & Identity: Redefining Meaning

Every person eventually faces a belief pivot—when the worldview or identity that once guided you no longer fits the person you've become. This could be spiritual, cultural, political, or philosophical. These pivots are sacred. They're not rebellion—they're awakening.

Notice: This belief feels more like a box than a compass. Decide: I have the right to outgrow narratives that no longer serve me. Move: Seek, read, meditate, listen without shame. Sustain: Build your belief system from experience, not expectation.

6. Location & Environment: Changing Your Scenery

A location pivot isn't just about geography—it's about energy. Different places, communities, or climates can completely reset your creativity, health, and sense of belonging.

Notice: I feel stuck and uninspired here. Decide: I deserve to live somewhere that supports my growth. Move: Test it first—travel, rent, explore. You don't have to sell everything tomorrow. Sustain: Create intentional rituals to stay connected to what matters, wherever you go.

"Sometimes the soil has nothing left for you. It's not failure to replant."

7. Friendships & Social Circles: Choosing Wisely

Not all friendships are meant to last forever. Some are meant for a season, a lesson, or a version of you that's no longer here. A friendship pivot means intentionally curating who gets access to your energy—not by becoming cold or exclusive, but by honoring mutual growth.

Notice: I leave this person's company feeling drained or small. Decide: It's okay to love people from a distance. Move: Quietly reduce energy investment; invest more in reciprocal connections. Sustain: Surround yourself with people who challenge and celebrate your evolution.

8. Family Dynamics: Breaking Generational Patterns

Family is the most emotionally complex arena. It's where we inherit not just DNA, but beliefs, coping styles, and unspoken rules. A family pivot doesn't mean cutting everyone off—it means consciously rewriting patterns that have silently run your life.

Notice: I'm repeating patterns that once hurt me. Decide: I can honor my family's story without reliving it. Move: Communicate boundaries with compassion, not rebellion. Sustain: Heal through example—change the pattern by living the new one. Family pivots heal not just you, but the generations that follow.

"You may be the first in your family to pivot—but not the last to benefit."

---

9. Creative & Purpose: From Productive to Expressive

Somewhere inside everyone is an artist—a creator, builder, or visionary waiting to breathe. A creative pivot is when you stop producing for approval and start creating for truth. Creativity isn't optional—it's the language of your soul.

Notice: I miss who I am when I'm creating. Decide: Even if no one sees it, this part of me deserves space. Move: Start with thirty minutes a day—paint, write, sing, design, build. Sustain: Protect your creative time as sacred. You don't have to monetize your creativity to legitimize it.

10. Lifestyle & Habits: Changing Your Daily Architecture

Sometimes the biggest life changes come from the smallest daily shifts. A lifestyle pivot might mean changing sleep patterns, technology use, routines, or the pace of your days. Because habits are the architecture of reality—they determine how your life feels when no one's watching.

Notice: I'm always rushing. I'm never present. Decide: I want a life that feels good, not just looks good. Move: Simplify. Slow down. Replace chaos with intentional structure. Sustain: Design your days around energy, not obligation.

11. Parenting & Legacy: Raising with Awareness

For parents, one of the most profound pivots is learning to parent more consciously—through example rather than control. Your children won't do what you say; they'll mirror what you model.

Notice: I'm reacting instead of responding. Decide: I want to raise through guidance, not guilt. Move: Apologize. Adjust. Begin again. Sustain: Model evolution—show them that adults can pivot too. Your parenting pivot might be the single greatest legacy you ever leave.

"When you pivot, your children inherit freedom instead of fear."

---

12. Purpose & Calling: From Success to Significance

At some point, you'll realize that success and significance are not the same. Success is about what you get. Significance is about what you give. This is the ultimate pivot—the shift from chasing achievement to creating impact.

Notice: I've achieved a lot, but I still feel empty. Decide: I want to live for contribution, not comparison. Move: Mentor. Volunteer. Create. Share your story. Sustain: Measure fulfillment by meaning, not metrics. This is where pivots become purpose—where personal transformation becomes collective impact.

13. The Inner Life: From Doing to Being

And finally, the deepest pivot of all. The inner life pivot is when you stop chasing external transformation and begin cultivating internal peace. It's the moment you realize your worth doesn't depend on your next move.

Notice: I'm addicted to progress. Stillness feels strange. Decide: I want peace, not just productivity.

Move: Meditate. Journal. Spend time in nature. Sustain: Let enough be enough. The final evolution of pivoting is presence—realizing that life isn't just about where you're going, but how deeply you can experience where you are.

"The final pivot is from chasing to cherishing."

A Final Case Study: From Resentment to Renewal (Age 84)

Eleanor is eighty-four. She lives with her husband in the same house they've owned for thirty years. Her health is fair, her finances stable—but her days feel heavy. Bitterness has crept in quietly. Behind her resentment lies something deeper: grief for the life she didn't fully live.

That's her Notice moment—the realization that her unhappiness isn't about others having more. It's about believing she's out of time to have enough.

One afternoon, her granddaughter visits and asks: Grandma, what makes you happiest to think about? Without thinking, Eleanor smiles. "Teaching. I loved helping young nurses when I worked at the hospital." That night, she writes in her journal: Maybe I'm not done teaching. Maybe I've just stopped offering. She decides her remaining time will be about giving, not comparing.

The next week, she calls a local nursing school and offers to volunteer. They pair her with first-year students. One says: You make it sound so simple—I wish you were my teacher every day. Something shifts. For the first time in years, Eleanor feels needed, alive, and seen.

She begins hosting a Tea & Tales group every Friday, inviting other seniors to share life lessons and laughter. Her envy dissolves as her energy expands. She tells her granddaughter: "I thought my story was finished. Turns out, I just stopped writing."

At any age, it's never too late to pivot from resentment to renewal. Fulfillment doesn't expire. It evolves.

Closing Thought

Whatever area you're considering—career, health, love, money, faith, or family—the same principle applies: when something feels off, you have permission to pivot.

You don't owe consistency to your past self. You owe authenticity to your present and future one. Every area of life can evolve. Every domain can align. Every decision, no matter how small, can change your trajectory.

The premise never changes: Notice. Decide. Move. Sustain.

EPILOGUE

Your Turn at the Line

When we began this journey, I told you that life is not linear—it's full of turns, forks, and choices. I shared how so many of us stay on autopilot, moving through routines without ever stopping to ask: Is this really my path?

By now, you've seen the cost of standing still, learned how to notice the signals, given yourself permission to decide, and built a plan to move and sustain. You've walked through the framework. But frameworks don't change lives. Action does.

The truth is, every pivot begins in a single moment: that instant where you recognize it's time to choose differently. That moment is now.

A Five-Minute Exercise

Grab a piece of paper, your phone's notes app, or the back of this book. Set a timer for five minutes. Write down:

Notice: One area of your life that feels misaligned—work, health, relationships, habits. Don't overthink it. Just notice it.

Decide: One choice you could make today that would move you closer to alignment. Not the big leap—just the decision to give yourself permission.

Move: One tiny step you could take in the next twenty-four hours. Send an email. Schedule a call. Sign up for a class. Journal the truth. Anything small, but real.

That's it. Five minutes. One area. One decision. One step. Because pivots don't start with blueprints, business plans, or bold announcements. They start here, in the quiet courage of a single act.

The line is drawn. The whistle is about to blow. It's your turn.

Closing Note

Your life is not predetermined. You are not bound to your past choices, your job title, or anyone else's expectations. You are free to pivot.

Every day, that freedom is renewed—in every decision, every yes and no, every whisper that says, This isn't it anymore.

You have one life. One shot at creating something true, aligned, and deeply your own. And one day, that life will look back at you. The only question will be: Did you live bravely enough to honor it?

I've always made myself one promise:

"I refuse to live my life in such a way where one day I may look back and say, 'What if?'"

What if is the language of regret. And regret is the price of standing still.

You don't have to have the perfect plan. You don't have to know where every road leads. You just have to choose motion—to trust that clarity is found in the movement, not before it.

So here you stand, your turn at the line. The world won't hand you permission. You have to claim it.

The question is not whether you can pivot.

The question is: Will you?

APPENDICES

Tools & Resources

Practical Frameworks to Move from Inspiration into Execution

Appendix 1: The Life Inventory Audit

Before you can pivot, you need clarity on where you are. This audit evaluates your alignment across six core life domains.

Set aside thirty quiet minutes. For each domain, rate yourself from 1 (low) to 10 (high) on both satisfaction and alignment, then answer the reflection questions.

Career: Do I wake up energized or drained by my work? Does it express my strengths and values? Relationships: Do the people around me support or suffocate my growth? Am I fully showing up? Health: Do my habits fuel energy or fatigue? How do I feel in my body most days? Finances: Are my money habits building freedom or feeding stress? Beliefs & Mindset: Are my current beliefs mine or inherited? Do they expand or limit me? Habits & Lifestyle: Which daily actions move me closer to the life I want—and which pull me away?

Circle the two lowest scores. These are your pivot starting points—the areas where small realignments can create outsized impact.

Appendix 2: The Discontent vs. Discomfort Grid

Growth hurts; misalignment drains. This exercise helps you tell the difference so you don't quit growth or cling to stagnation.

List three to five areas of life where you feel tension or unease. For each, answer: What does this feel like? Does this pain expand or deplete me? Is this a lesson I'm meant to learn, or a limitation I'm meant to leave? What's my next step—stretch or shift?

If the emotion feels alive, challenging, and purposeful, it's discomfort—keep growing. If it feels heavy, hopeless, and draining, it's discontent—time to pivot. Circle one true misfit. Commit to one concrete step toward change in that area within seven days.

Appendix 3: The Fear Map & Risk Budget

Fear loses power when defined. This exercise helps you map, measure, and manage your fears with logic instead of emotion.

Step One: Write every fear related to your potential pivot—rational or irrational. For each fear, identify the worst-case scenario, rate its likelihood from 1 to 10 and its reversibility from 1 to 10, and note one mitigation or antidote.

Step Two: Allocate your risk budget. Imagine risk as currency—you have 100 points to invest. Assign points to Career/Business, Finances, Relationships, Health, and Creative/Personal Growth. The goal isn't zero risk —it's smart risk, aligned with your priorities.

Step Three: For each high-fear, high-reward area, write one mitigation step you can take this week. Fear shrinks in proportion to movement.

Appendix 4: The Fulfillment Scorecard

Fulfillment is measurable. Use this scorecard monthly to track your internal metrics: Purpose, Energy, and Joy.

Once a month—the last Sunday works well—rate each category 1 to 10 and journal one sentence explaining why you chose that number. Calculate your average Fulfillment Index and note trends over time. When one metric trends down, treat it as a signal, not a shame.

Each quarter, choose one area to improve. Post your latest scorecard where you'll see it. Let awareness guide consistency, not guilt.

Appendix 5: The MAPP Assessment

Before you can pivot with purpose, you must know what drives you. The Motivational Appraisal of Personal Potential (MAPP)—available at Assessment.com—has helped more than twelve million people in over 170 countries uncover their core motivations, traits, stressors, and ideal environments. It takes about twenty minutes.

The MAPP reveals your motivational DNA: what drives your decisions (achievement, service, creativity, stability, influence), how you naturally think and problem-solve, what environments and tasks deplete your energy, and the specific conditions that make you feel most alive. Use your results to refine your Life Inventory Audit and strengthen your Pivot Thesis.

You can't fake fulfillment—but you can measure alignment. Know yourself deeply enough that every pivot feels like coming home.

Appendix 6: Your Pivot Permission Contract

There comes a moment when waiting becomes heavier than change itself. This is that moment.

Print this page, sign it in ink, and keep it somewhere visible—taped to your mirror, framed on your desk, or tucked into your journal—as a daily promise to honor your truth and live on purpose.

PIVOT PERMISSION CONTRACT

I hereby grant myself full and unconditional permission to pivot.

I recognize that my life is not predetermined. I am not bound by my past choices, my job title, my circumstances, or anyone else's expectations.

I will Notice when my soul signals it's time to change. I will Decide with clarity and conviction, even when uncertainty feels louder than confidence. I will Move with courage, taking imperfect action rather than waiting for perfect timing. I will Sustain my evolution with integrity, self-respect, and alignment.

I understand that standing still has a cost—in joy, energy, and time—and I refuse to let fear or comfort dictate the limits of my potential.

Above all, I make this vow to myself and to the one life I've been given:

> *"I refuse to live my life in such a way where one day I may look back and say, 'What if?'"*

Because I know that the only true failure is never finding out what could have been.

So today, I choose movement over stagnation. Faith over fear. Purpose over permission.

This is my turning point. This is my pivot. And it begins now.

Signature: ____________________ Date: ______________

Your Complimentary MAPP© Assessment

$89.95 Value — Included with Permission to Pivot

Limited to the first 100,000 readers who claim it.

You didn't pick up this book by accident. Something in your life—your career, your direction, your identity—no longer delivers what you truly need. This book gives you the framework to pivot. The MAPP© Assessment gives you the clarity to know where to go next.

Most people spend years—sometimes decades—guessing their way through life and work. The combination of this book and your MAPP© results gives you something most people never get: clarity, direction, and a framework to act.

What Is the MAPP© Assessment?

The MAPP© (Motivational Appraisal of Personal Potential) Assessment is one of the most trusted career assessments in the world, with over twenty-five years of use. Taken by more than 12,000,000 people, used in over 163 countries, translated into 15 languages, and utilized by 3,500+ professional coaches, it is designed to uncover your true motivations—not just your skills.

Instead of asking "What can you do?" the MAPP© reveals: **"What are you naturally wired to do, and enjoy?"**

You'll receive:

- Your top career matches
- The ability to match yourself with over 40,000 jobs
- Insight into your motivations and natural drivers
- Direction on careers, roles, degrees, and paths where you're most likely to thrive

How to Unlock Your MAPP© Results

Step 1: Create Your Account

Go to **www.assessment.com** and register for an Individual Account. Important: Business, Coach, or EDU accounts are not eligible for this offer.

Step 2: Take the MAPP© Assessment

Start and complete the MAPP© Assessment (approximately 15–20 minutes). This step is required to generate your results profile.

Step 3: Submit Your Claim

After completing the assessment, visit **assessment.com/permissiontopivot** and enter the same email address you used to create your Individual account, tell us where you purchased the book, and submit proof of purchase (order confirmation, receipt, or screenshot).

Step 4: Receive Your Keycode

Once verified, we will send a personal keycode to the email on your account. Use this keycode to unlock your full MAPP© Assessment results. Keycodes are one-time use only and valid for Individual accounts only.

Important Requirements

- Free MAPP® Assessment included with purchase of a physical book only; redemption requires a valid physical book purchase. eBook and audiobook purchases do not qualify.
- You must create an Individual Account at assessment.com
- You must complete the full MAPP© Assessment
- You must submit the same email used on your account
- Proof of purchase is required for verification
- Keycodes are one-time use only
- Business, Coach, and EDU accounts do not qualify
- Incomplete assessments will not receive access

Start Now

Go to **www.assessment.com**

Create your Individual account and complete the MAPP© Assessment.

Claim your results at
assessment.com/permissiontopivot

Your next chapter doesn't start with guessing.

It starts with knowing.

Continue the Journey

If this book resonated with you, this is just the beginning. I share real-time insights, stories, and examples of people and companies navigating their own pivots—across career, business, and life.

Follow along: **@WhatifPivot on Instagram**

www.ingramcontent.com/pod-product-compliance
Lightning Source LLC
LaVergne TN
LVHW091138080826
845145LV00008B/2186

* 9 7 8 1 9 6 9 8 2 6 5 5 9 *